ANGER MANAGEMENT

Edited by

R.N. Misra

DISCOVERY PUBLISHING HOUSE PVT. LTD.
NEW DELHI-110 002

Published by:
Tilak Wasan

DISCOVERY PUBLISHING HOUSE PVT. LTD.
4831/24, Prahlad Street, Ansari Road
Darya Ganj, New Delhi-110002 (India)
Phone: +91-11-23279245, 43764432
Fax: +91-11-23253475
E-mail: parul.wasan@gmail.com
info@discoverypublishinggroup.com
web: www.discoverypublishinggroup.com

***First Edition:* 2011**
ISBN: 978-81-8356-751-0

Anger Management

Printed at:
Shree Balaji Art Press
Delhi

Acknowledgements

I am thankful to all paper contributors for this book, it is not possible in my part to edit this book without their kind co-operation and in-time help for editing this book.

I would like to take this opportunity to thank my parents who helped me all the time for editing this book, firstly my wife Smt. Swarna Prava Misra need lot of thanks for this purpose. I thank my elder son Roopesh Kumar Misra and my daughter-in law Smt. Amrita Rani Misra. I would also like to thank my second son Mr. Rookesh Kumar Misra. This timely help and co-operation in editing this book.

Last but not least, a special word of thanks to Mr. Tilak Wasan, the Owner/Director of Discovery Publishing House (P) Ltd, New Delhi for publishing this book in time. I also place on record my sincere thanks to his son who is the real man for doing all publication work. Finally, I would like to thanks all members of publication division of Discovery Publishing House for their help and co-operation for publishing the book in time.

Prof. R.N. Misra

Preface

Anger is a natural emotion. Anger may include displeasure, irritation or dislike. When we react to frustration, criticism or a threat we become angry. Anger increases heart rate, blood pressure and other diseases. The external expression of anger can be found in facial expressions, body language physiological responses and at times in public acts of aggression. But the anger internally affects the body, damages nervues, make body discomforts, decrease efficiency, and creates many other problems.

In an organization anger plays a vital role for accomplishment of unproductive work, which seriously affect the workforce in a negative manner. So, management of Anger by the top to bottom mangers need due important in the present era. Anger management means the management of one's anger so that the least possible damage is felt to self, to others and management as whole. This involves understanding one's anger degree effectively and to take some steps to reduce his/her anger to a maximum level for the achievement of organisational goal. If a manger is able to control his/her anger successfully he will be able to manage the anger of his/her sub-ordinate. It is a technique to be adopted by the mangers by taking into pros and cons of all events into due consideration.

Prof. R.N. Misra

Contents

CHAPTER 1

Anger : How to Control?

Prof. R.P. Sarma*

> "The person who is angry at the right things and toward the right people, and also in the right way, at the right time and for the right length of time is morally praiseworthy."
>
> **—Aristotle**

Management is a very broad term and hence cannot be defined exactly. Any human activity handled by men for a specific achievement can be termed as management. Previously the tern widely used in connection with business management with the ultimate aim of earning profit. To-day the term is utilised in the meaning of "handle", "organise" "process" etc. with or without associating it with profit earning but an ultimate reaching the goal of individual or social system.

Hindu sages from the time of origin of human species tried to regulate the behaviour of mankind by prescribing certain fundamental principles which can be termed as "life management" for a decent life in this world and later in the unknown outer world, whether it may be Heaven of Hell on which we have no idea except certain imaginary concepts. According to Hindu scriptures man is composed of five

---

* Paul M. Hughes, *Anger,* Encyclopaedia of Ethics, Vol. I, Second Edition, Rutledge Press.

behaviours which are collectively called the human being. The physical body is not the man; man is identified by his behaviour.

There are five sensuous behaviour of man identified by the Hindu philosophers, which represents man, they are:

1. *Kama* or lust. It is one of the five fundamental behaviours that make man survive and progress in this world for pleasure and recreation. Men and women cannot live without this and the world cannot progress with out this.
2. *Krodha,* or anger. This is second fundamental behaviour which makes the men angry. It has no positive contribution to life instead has many harmful effect on life and makes the life unhappy.
3. *Lobha* or desire. Men cannot live without desire. To fulfil his or her desire human beings take up work in this world but too much of it is harmful.
4. *Mooha* or Attachment. An individual cannot remain aloof with out attachment to any particular aspect in the life. But to become a perfect man one has to try not to attach one-self intensively with any thing.
5. *Machharjya* or non-vegetarianism. The type of food one takes is also determines the nature of man and his behaviour. Those who are addict to non-vegetarian food and alcoholic drinks they are wilder in behaviour.

Men want to live in this world happily; happiness is a concept of mind and Hindu philosophers professed that if a man controls these five aspects of his behaviour the life will be happier in this world. And they advise to control all these five aspects as strongly as possible. Out of the five, the first one, lust is an important behaviour of man which is essential for life and for the progress of the society. To control this, Hindu sages prescribed certain laws. The most important of this law is the prescription of institution of "marriage" to control and regulate the behaviour of man and women in their sexual behaviour. Every religion has code of conduct to control *Kama or* sex behaviour. The essence of it is, love is for the procreation but not per se for physical enjoyment.

The five behavioural aspects of men is shown graphically in Fig. 1.1.

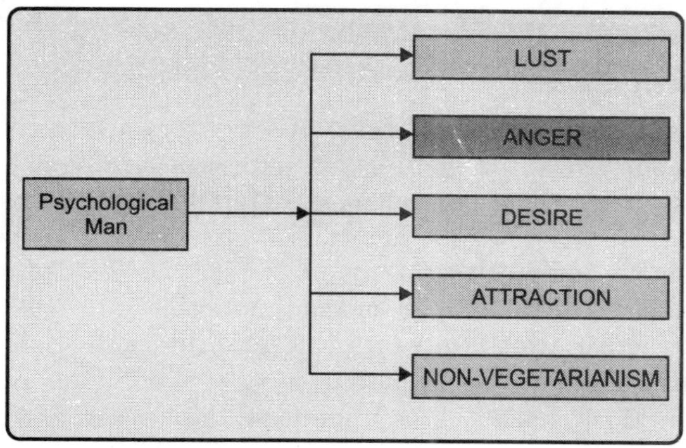

Fig. 1.1. The Psychological Man

Anger or Krodha

The second important behaviour of men is anger. The most important aspect of Anger is that it has no positive contribution to the life of human beings; it is always have negative effect on life. A life with out anger is most enjoyable in the society. On the other hand anger in its extreme case may destroy life itself. On the origin of anger Bhagabad Gita clearly mentions:

> *"Dhyayato vishayan pumsah samgasteshu pajayate,*
> *Sangatsajayate kamah kamatx kroodhobhijayathe"*
> Gita:2-62

When an individual thinks of a situation intensively originates attachment, attachment leads to desire and desire when remains unfulfilled it converts into anger. Anger gives birth to stupidity, which in turn disturbs the senses, when senses are disturbed it kills intellect and ultimately when intellect of a man is gone man is destroyed. Hence anger at last the cause of destruction of human beings.

The sequence of anger and destruction:

Intensive Attachment ⟶ Desire ⟶ Anger ⟶ Stupidity ⟶ Disturbing senses ⟶ Destruction

Modern Causes

Since anger has destructive quality in every aspects of life in recent years it is being given importance to manage it, that is, in true sense to control it. In family life, in social life or in business affairs it has to be controlled for harmony, happiness and profit respectively. Anger is a deluded mind that focuses on an animate or inanimate object, feels it to be unattractive, exaggerates its bad qualities, and wishes to harm it. The term anger management commonly refers to a system of psychological therapeutic techniques and exercises by which one with excessive or uncontrollable anger can control or reduce the degrees, and effects of an angered emotional state.

Modern psychologists mention eleven factors responsible for anger in a person. Every man faces such situations in which he became angry because of any one or more situation of this. For this he alone is responsible and responsible for his own destruction. Some realise later their fault but others never realise and remain under the grab of anger. The eleven causes of anger is briefly described below:

1. *Anxiety :* yes, anxiety is the birth of anger. One is very anxious to get certain result and in the process if he is not able to realise it or reach the goal expected he become enraged, looses his temper and dose some action which not expected by a normal person.
2. *Disappointment :* Men always aspire to get some thing in a situation but if they fail to achieve that he accuses others believing that they are responsible foe

the failure of his goal. Even if he knows that they are not directly responsible for his failure but blindly believe they are responsible and become angry on them.

3. *Embarrassment :* Some times for some action of an individual one faces embarrassment and even though it is no fault of others he become furious on others not realising he alone is responsible for that situation.
4. *Fear :* Fear is another factor for which a person not in a mood to think what to do in a situation when he is fearful. As he is not in a position to think what to do, he becomes angry on others at the spot or later.
5. *Frustration :* When one desires some thing and it is not attained then the person become frustrated. That leads to anger and blaming others or abusing self for not able to attained the desired results.
6. *Guilt :* When a person doing some work for him or for others not in a fair manner, sooner or later one feels guilty for the work done and repents for it. In this case also the person become angry and doses some thing not done by a sensible person.
7. *Hurt :* When a person feels hurt if some injustice is done to him physically or mentally he naturally become angry and takes revenge against the man or institution doing some harmful things.
8. *Jealousy :* When some possesses some thing but one is not in a position to acquire it for himself he become jealous. Under influence of jealousy he dose some action against the persons for whom he is jealous without any rational reason simply becoming angry.
9. *Sadness :* A person become sad if one is less rich less educated or has less social status in comparison to others. He cannot tolerate that others are higher to him in many respect for which he cannot do anything. Sadness some times silently reacts mentally dose some

work not expected for a rational human being under the influence of anger.

10. *Shame :* One feeling shameful for his status in the family, in the office or in the society may also converts into anger a he struggles to come out of that shameful state. In the process the anger may turn into wild behaviour in certain cases.
11. *Worry :* Psychologically some feel helpless for every work, big or small, and worry about it with out taking into account the realities. Many a time the worries seem false due to the misconception of the person. Feeling worry about the incident he becomes angry and try to abuse others in the process even though it us actually unnecessary.

Whether a head of the family or a manager of a business firm faces anger as a result of the above eleven factors; for a family anger disrupts family harmony and peace in the family while a manager who faces these if not control properly and restrain from anger the business firm is likely to be destroyed. Hence now a days the management pundits thinking seriously to restrain the managers from anger for better management practices and ultimately to earn good profit for the firm.

Can it be Controlled ?

Anger is one of the most common and destructive delusions, and it afflicts our mind almost every day. In order to control anger, one has to first recognize the anger within the mind, acknowledge how it harms both his self and others, and appreciate the benefits of being patient in the face of difficulties. Hence, one has to apply practical methods in daily life to reduce anger and finally to prevent it from arising at all.

Anger varies from person to person, the treatments are designed to be personal to the individual since it is based on an exaggeration, anger is an unrealistic mind; the intrinsically faulty person or thing that it focuses on does not in fact exist. Moreover anger is an extremely destructive mind that serves no useful purpose. Anger is "an emotional state that varies in intensity from mild irritation to intense fury and rage," Like other emotions, it is accompanied by physiological and biological changes; when you get angry, your heart rate and blood pressure go up, as do the levels of your energy hormones, adrenaline, and noradrenalin. Some simple methods prescribe are use of deep breathing and meditation to relax the mind.

Anger can be caused by both external and internal events. One could be angry at a specific person, such as a maid servant or supervisor or event such as a traffic jam or a cancellation of flight. Anger could be caused by worrying or brooding about personal problems. Memories of traumatic or enraging events can also trigger angry feelings. Anger is a natural, adaptive response to threats; it inspires powerful, often aggressive, feelings and behaviors, which allow us to fight and to defend ourselves when we are attacked. A certain amount of anger, therefore, is necessary to our survival. On the other hand, we can't physically lash out at every person or object that irritates or annoys us; laws, social norms, and common sense place limits on how far our anger can take us.

Three Approaches to Control

Anger cannot be controlled fully; the degree of it can be reduced to some extent. But the person who is very often become angry has to adopt certain procedure consciously to control it. No external remedies could cure anger of a person. There are certain procedures to be adopted to deal with angry feelings. There are three approaches one can try to control anger; they are (1) Expressing (2) Suppressing, and (3) Calming.

1. *Expressing :* Expressing one's angry feelings in an assertive, not aggressive, manner is the healthiest way to express anger. As one cannot fully control

anger one should try to use anger mildly with out using it much. For this one has to learn how to make one's view clear about what one needs, how to get them met, without hurting others. Being assertive doesn't mean being pushy or demanding; it means being respectful of yourself and others.

2. *Suppressing :* Anger when it comes can be suppressed, and then converted or redirected. This happens when one holds his anger, stop thinking about it, and focus on something positive. The aim is to inhibit or suppress the anger and convert it into more constructive behavior. The danger in this type of response is that if it isn't allowed outward expression, one's anger can turn inward, on one self. Anger turned inward may cause hypertension, high blood pressure, or depression. People who are constantly putting others down, criticizing everything, and making cynical comments haven't learned how to constructively express their anger. Not surprisingly, they aren't likely to have many successful relationships in life.
3. *Calming :* Finally, at the time of anger one can try to remain calm inside. This means not just expressing the outward behavior, but also controlling your internal responses, taking steps to lower heart rate, calm yourself down, and let the feelings subside. For this entire approaches one consciously have to try, no external advises or request to control anger help the angry person to reduce anger.

Why People Behave This Way?

Anger is a completely normal, usually healthy human emotion. But when it gets out of control and turns destructive, it can lead to problems—problems at work, in our personal relationships, and in the overall quality of one's life. The instinctive, natural way to express anger is to respond aggressively. Anger is a natural, adaptive response to threats;

it inspires powerful, often aggressive, feelings and behaviors, which allow us to fight and to defend ourselves when one is attacked. Hence, it is accepted that certain amount of anger is necessary in our life for survival. But beyond certain degree of anger is harmful to the person as well as to others and a hindrance to a happy life.

There is no specific answer why some people become angry. There are several causes for the behaviour of individuals in a particular emotional way. Different psychologists put different causes:

1. One cause may be anger is genetic or physiological: There is evidence that some children are born irritable, touchy, and easily angered, and that these signs are present from a very early age.
2. Anger may be socio-cultural. Anger is often regarded as negative aspect of mind; generally we are taught that expressing anxiety, depression, or other emotions are all right but not to express anger.
3. Parents are not conscious how to handle anger or channel it constructively. Family background plays an important role in regulating emotions.. Typically, it has been observed that people who are easily angered come from families that are disruptive, chaotic, and not skilled at emotional communications.
4. People who are easily angered generally have what some psychologists call a low tolerance for frustration, meaning simply that they feel that they should not have to be subjected to frustration, inconvenience, or annoyance. They can't take things in stride, and they're particularly infuriated if the situation seems somehow unjust: for example, being corrected for a minor mistake.

Goals of Anger Management

The goal of anger management is to reduce both emotional feelings and the physiological arousal that anger causes. One can't get rid of anger, or able to avoid it completely, the things or the people that neither enrage, nor can change them, but one can learn how to control ones reactions.

Relaxation is best Remedy

Relaxation is simplest mechanism to control anger. Simple relaxation tools, such as deep breathing and relaxing imagery, can help calm down angry feelings. There are many relaxation techniques, and once one learns the techniques, one can call upon them in any situation. If one is involved in a relationship where both partners are hot-tempered, it might be a good idea for both to learn these techniques. These are some of the simple steps one can try for relaxation.

- Breathe deeply, from diaphragm; breathing from chest won't relax one. Picture the breath coming up from your "gut."
- Slowly repeat a calm word or phrase such as "relax," "take it easy." Repeat it to yourself while breathing deeply.
- Use imagery; visualize a relaxing experience, from either your memory or your imagination.
- Non-strenuous, slow yoga-like exercises can relax muscles and make one feel much calmer.

Logic Defeats Anger

Anger, even when it's justified, can quickly become irrational. So use cold hard logic on yourself when your angry.. Remind yourself that the world is "not out to get you," you're just experiencing some of the rough spots of daily life. Do this each time you feel anger getting the best of you, and it will help you get a more balanced perspective. Angry people tend to demand things: fairness, appreciation, agreement, willingness to do things their way. Everyone wants these things, and one is hurt and disappointed when one don't get them, but angry people demand them, and when their demands aren't met, their disappointment becomes anger.

Humour Defuses Anger

"Silly humour" can help defuse rage in a number of ways. For one thing, it can help one to get a more balanced perspective. When one get angry and call someone a name or refer to them in some imaginative phrase, stop and picture what that word would literally look like. Angry people tend to feel that they are morally right, that any blocking or changing of their plans is an unbearable indignity and that they should not have to suffer this way.

There are two cautions in using humour. First, don't try to just "laugh off your problems; rather, use humor to help yourself face them more constructively. Second, don't give in to harsh, sarcastic humour; that's just another form of unhealthy anger expression. What these techniques have in common is a refusal to take you too seriously. Anger is a serious emotion, but it's often accompanied by ideas that, if examined, can make one laugh.

Some psychologists view anger in a different perspective and try to tackle it in a different way:

Selection of a suitable time : When one likely to face a situation which would bring a situation of anger, it is better to postpone it to some other time and avoid anger situation. If you and your spouse tend to fight when you discuss things at night, when you have returned tired at work in the office in a tense mod, try to changing the timing of discussion until the next morning the situation of anger can be prevented.

Try to Avoid the situation : Just by avoiding a situation anger can be stopped. If your child's chaotic room makes you furious every time you walk by it, then shut the door and avoid the situation. Don't make yourself look at what infuriates you. The point is to keep yourself calm in this situation and anger can be avoided.

Find the alternatives : If one's daily commute through traffic leaves you in a state of rage and frustration, then prepare an alternative rout your self which is less congested and more scenic. Or find another alternative, such as a bus or commuter train.

Strategies for Business Managers

Tension in the workplace is common. Everyone wants to be as productive as possible to improve their respective careers. This often creates a conflict of interest since a person wants to be on top over some employees—a fact that will not be received well by other employees who also wanted to improve in their career. Workplace competition, family problems, conflicting personalities and pressure from upper management could take its toll on employees. These factors could lead to frustration, stress and ultimately anger. Physical contact caused by anger could easily happen in the workplace if they are not prevented. Managers and supervisors have a big role in controlling anger and other forms of negative emotions on employees. As the leader, they have to take charge of every business aspect and everything that might affect the business process - including workplace turmoil among employees. When conflict escalates into anger in the workplace, the manager has to do all he can to prevent further damages in the workplace.

The reason why managers could be blamed for preventing such actions is that they are in a perfect position to implement strategies to prevent workplace violence and anger related problems. There are, in fact, specific strategies for managers to control and prevent anger in workplace. We can place these strategies into two types: the mild and strong strategies.

Mild strategy is all about seeking assistance as well as extending emotional help to the employees. Managers can ask company psychologist, psychiatrist and the Human Resource Department for evaluation and emotional assistance to their employees. Aside from outside help, managers could also control anger in their employees by implementing "assertive communication" wherein the manager expresses his or her feelings about the situation sternly with a fair reason why these feelings are triggered.

Strong Strategies are actual managerial actions that will control any confusion in the workplace and prevent rage. There are two things that a manager could do in this strategy. First is to specify the limitation for each employee. For example, each employee should provide an actual time-frame for the assignment so that the other employee would have fair expectations on how the project would be delivered. This expectation will be complemented by the second act a manager would do: penalization with a stern warning. Manager might run into employees that are not enthusiastic about the rules and expectations. This could create problems when they are not addressed as soon as possible. If they do not follow after a warning, penalization should be implemented.

Simple Steps for Gaining Control of Anger

William DeFoore's, some simple prescriptions for gaining control of anger are as follows :

- Breathe deep and long breaths. Be sure to open your belly and breathe deep into your abdomen. You may not know it, but when you are angry you're panicking. This will help you to calm down.
- Walk outside and look at the sky while you are doing your deep breathing. This will help you to put things in perspective, and it can have a soothing effect.
- Do some stretches. When a situation that makes you so angry, your body gets tense and rigid. The stretching will open up some of the tight areas of your body and get more oxygen flowing to your brain and help you clear your thoughts.
- Get some paper and start writing. Write about how mad you are and why. Don't be nice, reasonable or rational. The point is to get your anger out on the paper, to purge it from your mind. Keep writing until you feel some relief or release, and don't stop until you do.

- Write about what you have to be grateful for, what you appreciate about your life, your self and also the person you are mad at.
- Imagine that you are at the funeral of the person you are mad at. What would you say? What would you miss about that person if they were gone?
- If you know how to pray, pray for God to guide you through this dark time. Pray for the grace to see the beauty and vulnerability in the person you are mad at. Pray for the wisdom to see beyond the view of the person.
- Imagine that you are the person you are mad at. Put yourself in their shoes. Look at the situation from their viewpoint. How do you look to them? Is that how you want to look? Decide who and how you want to be and act as if you were that already.
- Remember a time in your childhood when you were afraid, hurt or angry. In your imagination, embrace that child, saying "It's okay. I'm here. You didn't do anything wrong. You're a good kid. I love you" then in your imagination take the child out of the situation to a safe place where she/he can relax, heal or even play.
- Think about your values. What is the most important thing in the world you love? Who are the most important people in the world to you? What kind of person do you want to be? How do you want to be remembered? Decide that you are that person and you are living by your values, and act as if it were so. This is the fastest way to change your emotions, and it puts you in touch with your true Self, the way you were designed to be.

These tips are not exhaustive; these are ten tips, or so to say "Ten Commandments" only. If one wants to control anger one has to try sincerely then good results would come out of it which would be good for the self and also good for the world.

Conclusion

Anger is one of the fundamental behaviour of human beings which has mostly harmful aspects. If one likes to live happily in the world one has to control anger in every situation faced by him in the world in day to day life. Whether as a father, husband or a manager of firms in order to smooth running of affairs with self-prestige one has to control anger and follow some of the prescriptions by Gurus and psychologists. No body would help you; you alone have to help yourself.

REFERENCES

- Anger, (Hindu Dharma: Dharmas Common To All), Shri Kanchi Kamakoti Peetham.
- Veylanswami, Satguru Bodhinatha, Anger Management: How to Tame our Deadliest Emotion.
- Beck, Richard; Richard Beck and Ephrem Fernandez (1998). "Cognitive-Behavioral Therapy in the Treatment of Anger: A Meta-Analysis". *Cognitive Therapy and Research 22* (1): 63-74.
- Burkeman (2006) Anger Management. Geddes, D. & Callister, R. 2007 Crossing The Line(s): A Dual Threshold Model of Anger in Organizations, *Academy of Management Review*. 32 (3): 721-746.
- Glomb, T. M. 2002. Workplace anger and aggression: Informing conceptual models with data from specific encounters. *Journal of Occupational Health Psychology*, 7: 20-36.
- Haque, Amber (2004), "Psychology from Islamic Perspective: Contributions of Early Muslim Scholars and Challenges to Contemporary Muslim Psychologists", *Journal of Religion and Health* 43 (4): 357-377 [367].
- Harris, W., Schoenfeld, C. D., Gwynne, P. W., Weissler, A. *M.,Circulatory and humoral responses to fear and anger, The Physiologist*, 1964, 7, 155.
- Fiero, John W., *Anger,* Ethics, Revised Edition, Vol. 1.
- Leland, R. Beaumont, Emotional Competency, Anger, An Urgent Plea for Justice and Action, Entry describing paths of anger.

- Sinaceur, M, LZ Tiedens, Get mad and get more than even: When and why anger expression is effective in negotiations, *Journal of Experimental Social Psychology,* 2006.
- Novaco, R. (1975). Anger control: The development and evaluation of an experimental treatment. Lexington, MA: Heath.
- Hall, Parker, 2008, *Anger, Rage and Relationship: An Empathic Approach to Anger Management,* Routledge, London.
- Desmond Morris, *Primate Ethology*, 1967, (Ed.). Weidenfeld & Nicolson Publishers: London, p. 55.
- DiGiuseppe, Raymond and Raymond Chip Tafrate, *Understanding Anger Disorders,* Oxford University Press, 2006, pp. 133-159.
- Kemp, Simon, K.T. Strongman, Anger theory and management: A historical analysis, *The American Journal of Psychology*, Vol. 108, No. 3. (Autumn, 1995), pp. 397-417.
- Tiedens, Ellsworth and Mesquita, *Sentimental Stereotypes: Emotional Expectations for High-and Low-Status Group Members,* 2000.
- Tiedens, L. Z. 2000. Powerful emotions: The vicious cycle of social status positions and emotions. In N. M. Ashkanasy, C. E. J. Ha" rtel, & W. J. Zerbe (Eds.), *Emotions in the workplace: Research, theory and practice:* 71-81. Westport, CT: Quorum.
- Tiedens, LZ, Anger and advancement versus sadness and subjugation: the effect of . negative emotion expressions on social status conferral, Link: [1], *Journal of Personality & Social Psychology*, 2001 Jan; 80(I): 86-94.
- Kleef, Van, De Dreu and Manstead, The Interpersonal Effects of Anger and Happiness in Negotiations, *Journal of Personality and Social Psychology,* 2004, Vol. 86, No. 1, 57-76.
- Wang, Xiaoling, Ranak Trivedi, Frank Treiber, and Harold Snieder, Genetic and Environmental Influences on Anger Expression, John Henryism, and Stressful Life Events: The Georgia Cardiovascular Twin Study, *Psychosomatic Medicine* 67:16-23 (2005).

CHAPTER 2

Anger Management

Sanjeev Tripathy*

Introduction

Anger is something that everyone in life will experience. Anger is completely normal. It is usually a healthy human emotion. However, when it gets out of control it can lead to problems, e.g. Problems at work, in our personal lives, relationships, and overall can impact on the quality of our lives.

When an angry episode occurs all of the following are involved:

- Cognition—our present thoughts
- Emotion—the physiological arousal our anger produces
- Communication—the way we display our anger to others
- The affect of anger on others—fear, hostility
- Behaviour—the way we behave when we are angry

We also, if we are aware of it, feel the results of anger in our own bodies. According to psychologists who specialize in anger management, there are some people who are angrier than others. They usually become angry more easily and more intensely than the average person. There are also some people that do not show their anger in loud spectacular ways

* Faculty in Marketing, PGCMS, SMIT, Ankeshpur, Berhampur, Orissa.

but are chronically irritable and grumpy. These people usually withdraw socially and/or become physically ill.

The physical signs/symptoms of anger :

- Tension or stress begins to build eg. easily frustrated, clenched posture
- Breathing rate increases
- Blood pressure rises *e.g.,* Flushed face/neck, veins standing out

The effects of anger on our health :

- Headaches - creates more tension and stress
- Stomachache
- Skin rash
- Arthritis - anger produces uric acid in the bloodstream which contributes to the onset of arthritis
- Circulatory disorders
- Aggravation of existing physical symptoms
- Emotional disturbances
- Suicide and murder

The Causes of Anger

There are a number of causes of anger. One cause might be genetic or physiological. There is evidence that suggests that some children are born with irritable, sensitive, and easily angered natures and these signs are present from a very early age. Another cause might be our fast paced and increasingly pressured way of life.

Because anger is often regarded as negative, we are taught that it is all right to express anxiety or depression and all other emotions but not anger. This can result in outbursts from a buildup of tension.

It may also be a result of frustration from our experiences in life, a disturbed background and/or our lifestyle. People often learn to react with anger from their parents.

Other Sources of Aanger

1. *Inadequacy in Family Life :*
   (*a*) Little contact with your family or if you feel you do not get enough direction from your family members, especially parents!
   (*b*) Exposure to Violence at home
   (*c*) Expectations or attitudes at home that encourage violence.
2. *Neighborhood:* Neighborhoods that have a high rate of crime are most prone. However, if you have nothing to do in your neighborhood this could also be a source of anger. In other words, when people say I did nothing yesterday and mean it!
3. *School and Peers:* Problems in this area can lead to a great deal of stress. Many times, these new relationships are not monitored by an adult and can lead to violent confrontations.
4. *Alcohol, illicit drugs and firearms:* How is this source of anger? Well everyone needs an escape from stress. The combination of these factors can lead to irrationality. Let's face it. Someone with a firearm who has been drinking or using drugs is not a formula for a healthy environment.
5. *Adolescence-Adulthood Transition:* It is a stressful time trying to understand what you want to do with your life and who you want to be.

Link between Anger and Mental Illness

The prevalence of anger attacks, defined as irritability, inappropriate anger and rage, frequent outbursts and overreaction to minor annoyances in patients with depression can be as high as 44 per cent. Also people with bipolar disorder can have episodes or periods of irritability when hypomanic or manic.

Treatment for Anger

It is potentially dangerous to 'let it rip' with anger as it escalates the anger and aggression and does nothing to help us or the person we are angry with.

Solutions for Anger Management

- One strategy is to find out what it is that triggers our anger then maybe develop strategies to keep those triggers from tipping you over the edge.
- Another strategy is relaxation, which is very important for our body to relax and breathe deeply. Picture your breath coming up from your 'gut'.
- Slowly repeat a calm word or phrase, for example "take it easy", and repeat it to yourself while breathing deeply.
- Non-strenuous, slow yoga-like exercises can also relax muscles and bring feelings of calmness.
- Cognitive refraining - changing the way we think - can work. Try to replace the exaggerated and overly dramatic angry thoughts with more rational ones, for example, telling yourself 'Oh well, I know it's terrible, it's frustrating and it's understandable that I'm upset but oh well, it's not the end of the world and anger is not going to fix anything'.
- Develop better communication skills. Sometimes angry people tend to jump to and act on conclusions, these are not always very accurate. It is important to have slower discussions with others. Also, think through your responses. Do not say the first thing that comes into your head and think carefully about what you want to say, and at the same time, listen to what the other person is saying.
- Changing your environment, for example, sometimes our immediate surroundings give cause for anger. Give yourself a break making sure that you have some

"personal time" scheduled for times in the day that you know are particularly stressful.

- Counselling may be needed if you think that your anger is out of control. Psychologists or other licensed mental health professionals can help work with anger by developing a range of techniques for changing thinking and behavior. This can be surprisingly effective - even by just admitting to a problem and being willing to change is a big step in the right direction - as frightening as that may be.
- Assertiveness training may help. Some angry people need to learn to become assertive at a point well before the anger is triggered. The aim of developing assertiveness is for people who do not express themselves well on a daily basis.

Goals of Anger Management

- Developing better communication skills with the aim of improving relationships
- Developing an understanding of what triggers anger
- Developing strategies to deal with anger
- Developing listening skills
- Developing skills like 'refraining' negative thoughts about life situations
- Getting help to change your life circumstances
- Stress management
- See your local GP or have an assessment conducted by a mental health professional - a GP can advise/ refer you
- Counseling and therapy, in particular Cognitive Behavioral Therapy and alternative therapies

Conclusion

The Power of Autosuggestion Think positive. We become what we think. We can strength ourselves emotionally by seeking support from outside factors, as mentioned earlier, and also by seeking support from our own self. This is known as therapy through autosuggestion.

Autosuggestion means consciously giving yourself positive messages that boost your self-confidence and make you emotionally strong.

Autosuggestion does not mean self denial or self- delusion. Lying to you will not help. Escapism never works. Autosuggestion means telling yourself that you have done your best and will continue to do so. Through this self-interaction

Tell yourself:

- I can do this.
- I have done my part of the duty.
- This is what I have achieved.

This should be your spirit, to continue with struggle, determined that you would never surrender. Once that determination is ingrained in your psyche, that you would never accept defeat, the threshold level of the survival instinct would rise. You should continuously keep strengthening yourself emotionally by giving similar message to yourself.

Coin your positive slogans :

- I will always remain strong.
- I will always continue to fight.
- I will never accept defeat.
- I will never lose hope.
- I will never break down.
- I will never give up.

Spirituality

Now we will discuss how we can manage anger spiritually. Emotions followed the development of intellect and, finally, the spiritual or philosophical aspect of human beings developed. It is this philosophical aspect that distinguishes man most clearly from lesser animals.

What is Philosophy?

Action is a must to sustain life. We all act. But do we ever pause and think about what exactly is going on? About why we act the way we do? And what is the end purpose of all these activities is?

In order to understand the underlying cause of actions that are taking place around us, we need to have a philosophical perspective.

Following are the steps to be taken in the spiritual way of anger managament:

- Think that everything is temporary.
- Life is a short journey on earth.
- Nothing is really very important.
- Everything is not in our hand.
- Why to ponder over loss when you did not bring anything on earth.

CHAPTER 3

Anger Management and Employee Burnout

H. Srinivas Rao*

Introduction

Anger is a deluded mind that focuses on an animate or inanimate object, feels it to be unattractive, exaggerates its bad qualities, and wishes to harm it. For example, when we are angry with out partner, at that moment he or she appears to us as unattractive or unpleasant. We then exaggerate his bad qualities by focusing only on those aspects that irritate us and ignoring all his good qualities and kindness, until we has built up a mental image of an intrinsically faculty person. We than wish to harm him in some way, probably by criticizing or disparaging him.

Importance of the Study

This is an emerging area. Hence, the present topic is a modern one and assumes significance.

Objectives

To achieve the main purpose and to give direction to the paper the following objectives are set forth :

(*i*) To review the merging HR Practices in the new milieu.

* Sr. Lecturer in Commerce, Badruka College of Commerce, Kachiguda, Hyderabad-27, Andhra Pradesh.

(*ii*) To highlight the impact of employee burnout, anger emotions.

(*iii*) To identify individual anger reasons.

(*iv*) To suggest the anger management techniques as per the *yoga* system.

Data and Methodology

Secondary data for the purpose of present study are compiled from different published sources and the primary data are based on the personal observations in the filed.

Anger Management in Times of Recession

With mounting work pressure and layoffs during time of recession, anger among the employees is on the rise. Anger is an extremely destructive emotion that affects the professional as well as personal lies of employees. In such a situation, employees need to learn how to control their anger. The management also needs to tackle it and show sympathy towards such employees who are buckling under work pressure, supporting and motivating them for better performance and help dispel their anger feelings.

Individual Anger Reasons

- Physical and mental problems in adjusting to the demands and constrains of work.
- Inability to cope up with change and its speed.
- Perceived job insecurity.
- Extreme fear or stress and spiritual void.
- Health problems, drug abuse and alcoholic behavior.
- Unreasonable expectations.
- Emotional reasoning of small and normal events.
- Memories of past traumatic and enraging events like intimidation by others, mistreatment by the supervisors.

- Aggressive and retaliatory nature of employees.
- Chronic problems—angry with themselves.
- Poor judgmental capabilities of staff over others intention and behavior.
- Long hours of frustration and stress.
- Absence of optimistic mindset.
- Procrastination of work till deadline for completion.

The study also disclosed some of the uncontrollable factors contributing to the anger of the employees in the workplace.

Anger Due to Uncontrollable Factors

- Uncomfortable surrounding causing frustration and stress.
- Intimidation and injustice by the management.
- Mistreatment and humiliation by superiors.
- Job insecurity and continuously changing nature of job.
- Hurtful criticisms and conflict between employees.
- Betrayal of employees' trust and ignoring their genuine needs.
- Unreasonable attack on employees and their ides.
- Disturbing situations like abuse, irritation and unfairness.
- Lack of outside support.

There are a number of anger management strategies available, the effectiveness of many of them has not yet been proved. What is effective and useful to one, may not help others. Depending upon the level of anger and the frequency in which it arises, employees will have to select a model that best suits them. Tony Fiore and Ari Novick in their most acclaimed book, '*Anger Management for 21st Century*' suggested a set of eight-key anger management tools. They are listed below:

- Recognize stress before it turns into anger.
- Develop empathy by seeing things from other perspective and willing to listen.
- Respond to anger (through appropriate methods) rather than reacting to it. Getting anger hardly solves anything.
- Recognize and modify the inner conversation to determine how to express anger.
- Communicate with others assertively without getting hostile to anybody or anything.
- Learn to adjust expectations according to reality.
- Do not forget things but forgive others.
- Retreat and think things are over by taking temporary time out from the situation.

All these steps are interactive in nature and very useful in relating tension in the present cut-throat work environment. However, in the heat of the moment, it can be hard for employees to remember and adopt to these copying strategies and skills. It may take some time and require few intense efforts to put these techniques into practice. In order to keep the anger under control and manage it properly, the following other strategies are also recommended:

- *Relaxation*: By deep breathing, reading relaxation books and by other methods.
- *Problem solving*: By finding ways to face the problem instead of avoiding it.
- *Cognitive Restructuring*: By changing the way people think.
- *Humor and Joy*: By motivating a sense of happiness to lighten angry feelings.
- Improving working conditions.

- Flexible working hours.
- Measure Employee satisfaction.
- Conduct *yoga*, Naturopathy Camps
- Recognising and rewarding the good work of employees.

Stress at Work

Stress had become a part and parcel of human life affecting the health of both, the employee and the organization. Though it is a negative consequence of modern living, it is not necessarily bad and of itself. There is also a positive side to stress, called eu-stress generating healthy and constructive responses to stress. This paper highlights the positive impact of stress in our life and on the level of performance at work. It reveals that optimum level of stress is required for the well-being of an individual and for the survival of an organization.

Sings of Employee Burnout

- *Excessive Absenteeism*: When a disciplined employee suddenly starts taking excess leaves or starts reporting late for work, this could point either to his professional or personal problems.
- *Lack of Quality and Quantity in Work*: When an employee feels depressed or dissatisfied with this work, the quality of his work decreases.
- *Lack of interest*: When a dedicated employee levels the office on time without finishing his work, it clearly shows his/her negligence towards the job.
- *Misbehaviour*: Sometimes, dissatisfied and depressed colleagues start misbehaving with fellow employees.
- *Complains by Employees*: Dissatisfied employees put forward many complaints to the HR Department regarding salary, working conditions, employee benefits, working hours, etc.

Reasons for Employees Burnout

- *Excess Workload*: Excess workload is the main reason of employee burnout. An employee performs many responsibilities at the same time which leaves him / her totally exhausted. A professional has to meet clients and council them, conduct trails and, in some cases, needs to counsel the relatives of the parent.
- *Work Environment*: The employees have to work in tight work environment, which is tough. The employees work in shift schedules and the changing shifts take a toll on an employee's health.
- *Emotional Involvement*: The job involves a lot of emotional involvement form the workers' side. During a trial process generally the employees get emotionally attached to the work. Such kind of emotional involvement leaves employees stressed.
- *High Exposure to Infection*: Employees work in an environment where they are continuously exposed to many types of problems. Clients come with different types of diseases and sometimes they infuse these problems to the staff.
- *Occupational Allergies*: In any profession, various occupational allergies are involved. These allergies make employees stressed and if they keep on getting allergies at regular intervals, it makes them stressed and depressed.
- *Violence Towards Healthcare Workers*: Violence towards employees is anther reason of stress. The professionals are involved in matters of life and death.
- *Work Organization and Health*: The way in which work is organized in organizations has a significant impact on the health of employees.
- *Lock of Rewards and Recognition*: Lac of rewards and recognition for good work is also a reason of employee burnout, when the top management of the

organisation does not recognize and reward the good work of employees, they may feel that they are not doing anything good for the organization.

Impact of Employees Burnout

- *Low Productivity*: When an employee is depressed dissatisfied, naturally his productivity deteriorates and the quality of the work suffers. He will not be able to provide the right kind of service to clients.
- *Poor Employee Morale*: Employee burnout leads to poor employee morale, which ultimately has an impact on employee performance.
- *High Employee Turnover Cost*: A depressed employee quits earlier than a satisfied employee. The burnout is a major factor in high employee turnover cost. Mostly, nurses and other junior level employees quit sooner because of depression and excess work load.

Overcoming the Problem of Employee's Anger and Burnout

- *Introduce Employee Stock Operation*: Introduction of stock operations among the employees will create a form of willingness and commitment towards work. Employees will work seriously when they see that their activities are going to increase or decrease their income.
- *Commitment of the Employees to Health promotion and disease management programs*: Committing employees to healthcare and disease management programs will make them more conscious about their health and fitness. Employees will keep themselves fit to perform well on their respective jobs.
- *Free Acupuncture*: Providing free facility of acupuncture services in the hospital will help the employees to become stress free, as well as increase their productivity and accuracy in crucial operations.

- *Timely Team Meetings*: Calling timely team meetings of employees and discussing various work related issues with the professions helps the employees in distressing, as well as giving an indication to the employees that the higher authorities are caring for them. These meetings also serve as an instrument of feedback to the management.
- *Flexible Working Hours*: To reduce the stress of employees, the organization also give flexible working hours. However, the flexibility cannot be given to everybody. So, the employees who have some problems working at regular hours can be given working hours of their choice. Flexible working hour are particularly helpful for staff and junior level staff.
- *Identify Gaps Across Organizational Levels and Functions*: it will be very useful for hospitals to identify that gaps at various organizational levels and functions. This information will help management fill the gap between various organizational levels. It will also reduce the work pressure and stress of overloaded employees. Further, this exercise will increase the overall efficiency of employees and will lead to providing better service to clients.
- *Conduct Yoga, Naturopathy*: Frequent *yoga* and naturopathy camps help employees distress. Yoga is an effective way of exercising as well as it helps a person to calm down. In naturopathy camps, various natural herbs are used to relax and calm down a person.
- *Recognizing and Reworking the Good Work of employees*: Recognizing the good work of employees is a good way to improve their productivity and morale. Rewarding and recognizing the work of employees helps them distress and motivates other to work hard to get the same kind of rewards and recognition.

Revisiting the HR Function

As the pace of change is increasing, organizations are trying to find new ways to compete effectively. Now, there are raised expectations even about the services that the HR function provides in organizations. The HR function is expected to be an active contributor in fulfilling strategic organizational needs. The re-engineered role of HR in the changing scenario needs serious discussion.

Emerging HR in the New Milieu

Human resources are the mighty pillars that form the business colonnade in today's world where a clear upswing the firm's aim for district competitive advantage is evident. The paper discusses the revolutionized state of affairs and its impact on Human Resource Management (HRM), its new role, emerging trends for a more adaptable, and customer-centered HRM. In this turbulent competitive era, staying abreast demands a paradigm shift in Human Resource Development (HRD). Recession is a recent turnaround in the business environment. The present work highlights the visible blow of recession on HRD and its approaches to deal with the same. 'Human factor's is a mantra for an organization's survival and progress.

Emerging Trends

Combating the latest trends and competition in business environment globally, requires human resources as an important asset for the organizations. With the change in all the facts of life—new trends, frames and attitudes are developing in the fields of applied HR Management.

Combating the Latest Trends and Competition in Business Environment

An effective performance management systems to match the compensation policies with HR Policies, TCS, for e.g. has a Sales Incentive Compensation Management and is increasingly becoming the key decisive and motivating factor in influencing sales force execution to impact business performance.

HR Scorecard Approach to align HR Systems with the company's overall strategy. Composite Cross cultural Training – Reliance Energy Ltd. Emphasizes T & D as the core functions to bridge the gap between the changing requirements of the ob and the abilities that individuals need to perform these takes such as self-directed leadership, self-motivated terms and self generated creativity to excel.

Corporate social responsibility, employee relations management, corporate transformation, talent management/ engagement, employee Assistance Program, Flexible Work Option (FWO), HR outsourcing, multi-level performance analysis: people, teams, the organization, are also initiatives taken on the part of HR system by virtue of the changing trends in the market. Now just new ideas and their implementation, it is essential that the organization believes in the efforts made and the values that are shared across the organization.

Conclusion

Employee burnout and Anger is becoming a common issue in organizations around the word. Depression, high rates of injury and prolonged absence from work is becoming feature of work in the companies. All costs have a direct impact on the employees abilities to deliver efficient and high quality services. Organizations need to develop the right kind of programs to handle the burnout problem of their employees. By taking effective measures, organizations can handle the burnout problem of employees. For recruiting and retaining good talent for the companies any sector needs to create and maintain a healthy workplace.

Organizations should pay more attention to the well-being of their employees and ease the emotional burden of people. Besides, the employees must understand that winning is not everything' in life. They should not struggle to achieve perfection in all tasks: after all no one is perfect in this world. They have to realize that the price for winning is very high in though times. They have to look into other dimensions of life by appreciating and enjoying things beyond work.

When they know how to fix things in place, it becomes a easier for them. The recent slowdown has a bad domino effect across the globe and has not been favourable for the employees. Darwin's "Survival of the Fittest" theory rings true in today's corporate context. Anger is the perfect time when employees come to know how much strong they are and how fast they can respond to difficult situations. Employees are incharge of their careers. Thus, they should work towards making their jobs anger free, interesting and enjoyable.

REFERENCES

- *HRM Review*, IUP Publications [2010]
- *HRM Review*, ICFAI University Press [2009]
- *Business India*—The Magazine of the Corporate World [2010]
- *Global Economy and Global Managers*, ICFAI University Press [2008]

CHAPTER 4

Anger Management

Dr. Ch. Tirupathi Rao*

Introduction

We all know what anger is, and we've ail felt it: whether as a fleeting annoyance or as full-fledged rage.

Anger is a completely normal, usually healthy, human emotion But when it gets out of control and turns destructive, it can lead to problems—problems at work, in your personal relationships, and in the overall quality of your life. And it can make you feel as though you're at the mercy of an unpredictable and powerful emotion. This brochure is meant to help you understand and control anger.

What is Anger?

Anger is a deluded mind that focuses on an animate or inanimate object, feels it to be unattractive, exaggerates its bad qualities, and wishes to harm it. For example, when we are angry with our partner, at that moment he or she appears to us as unattractive or unpleasant. We then exaggerate his bad qualities by focusing only on those aspects that irritate us and ignoring all his good qualities and kindness, until we

* Reader in Commerce, Government Degree & P.G. College (Men), Srikakulam-532001, Andhra Pradesh.

have built up a mental image of an intrinsically faulty person. We then wish io harm him in some way, probably by criticizing or disparaging him.

Because It is Based on an Exaggeration, Anger is An-unrealistic Mind

Because it is based on an exaggeration, anger is an unrealistic mind; the intrinsically faulty person or thing that it focuses on does not in fact exist. Moreover, as we shall see, anger is also an extremely destructive mind that serves no useful purpose whatsoever. Having understood the nature and disadvantages of anger, we then need to watch our mind carefully at all times in order to recognize it whenever it begins to arise.

This explanation of how to overcome our anger through practising patience is based on Guide to the Bodhisattva's Way of Life, the famous poern by the great Buddhist Master Shantideva. Though composed over a thousand years ago, this is one of the clearest and most powerful explanations of the subject ever written, and is just as relevant today as it was then.

Anger is a natural emotion. It's nature's way of telling us that something in our lives has gone haywire. Anger occurs as a defensive response to a perceived attack or threat to our well-being. In addition to psychological changes, like any emotion, anger is accompanied by physiological changes. When you get angry your adrenaline flows, your heart rate increases, and your blood pressure escalates. The phrase, "I'm so mad my blood is boiling" isn't that far from true when you fly into a rage!

Sometimes just our perception of a situation causes anger to ignite and sometimes the threat may be real. Whatever the case, anger isn't the problem. The problem with anger is that many of us don't learn to manage anger effectively. In fact, one out of five Americans has an anger management problem.

Domestic abuse, road rage, workplace violence, divorce, and addictions are a few of the external examples of the results of poor anger management. Moreover, anger can lead to physical problems when not properly managed. Long-term anger has been linked to chronic headaches; sleep disorders, digestive problems, high blood pressure, and even heart attack.

Yet, when you learn how to manage anger, it can be an accelerant towards positive change instead of a negative propeller towards disaster.

The Sequence of Anger

Anger is usually "triggered" by an occurrence, like stubbing your toe on an inanimate object or by something that someone says. Next, you think something like "what did I do to deserve that". However, at this point, emotion takes over your mind and the "pain" of the situation leads you to believe the answer to your question is "Nothing. I didn't deserve that at all!" Feelings of hurt and betrayal further try to override logic and you're ready to act on your anger by either suppressing it or expressing it.

Suppressing your anger may lead you to believe you have it under control. However, suppressing anger doesn't solve your problem and is a dangerous type of anger management. Suppressed anger stays with you over time and can lead to mental health problems like depression, and physical problems like "stress" headaches and high blood pressure. Additionally, continually suppressing your anger can curtail your ability to act in the face of a real threat to your well-being.

Anger needs to be expressed. Yet, aggressive displays of anger can.result in violent eruptions that further hurt you socially, mentally, and physically. The goal of anger management is to help you find healthy ways to express your anger and resolve the problems that ignite it. The first step in anger management is learning to define the problem and face it head on!

The Nature of Anger

Anger is "an emotional state that varies in intensity from mild irritation to intense fury and rage," according to Charles Spiel Berger, PhD, a psychologist who specializes in the study of anger. Like other emotions, it is accompanied by physiological and biological changes; when you get angry, your heart rate and blood pressure go up, as do the levels of your energy hormones, adrenaline, and nor adrenaline.

Anger can be caused by both external and internal events. You could be angry at a specific person (such as a coworker or supervisor) or event (a traffic jam, a canceled flight), or your anger could be caused by worrying or brooding about your personal problems. Memories of traumatic or enraging events can also trigger angry feelings.

Expressing Anger

The instinctive, natural way to express anger is to respond aggressively. Anger is a natural, adaptive response to threats; it inspires powerful, often aggressive, feelings and behaviours, which allow us to fight and to defend ourselves when we are attacked. A certain amount of anger, therefore, is necessary to our survival.

On the other hand, we can't physically lash out at every person or object that irritates or annoys us; laws, social norms: and common sense place limits on how far our anger can take us.

People use a variety of both conscious and unconscious processes to deal with their angry feelings. The three main approaches are expressing, suppressing, and calming. Expressing, your angry feelings in an assertive—not aggressive—manner is the healthiest way to express anger. To do this, you have to learn how to make clear what your needs are, and how to get them met, without hurting others. Being assertive doesn't mean being pushy or demanding; it means being respectful of yourself and others.

Anger can be suppressed, and then converted or redirected. This happens when you hold in your anger, stop thinking about it, and focus on something positive. The aim is to inhibit or suppress your anger and convert it into more constructive behavior. The danger in this type of response is that if it isn't allowed outward expression, your anger can turn inward—on yourself. Anger turned inward may cause hypertension, high blood pressure, or depression.

Unexpressed anger can create other problems. It can lead to pathological expressions of anger, such as passive-aggressive behaviour (getting back at people indirectly, without telling them why, rather than confronting them head-on) or a personality that seems perpetually cynical and hostile. People who are constantly putting others down, criticizing everything, and making cynical comments haven't learned how to constructively express their, anger. Not surprisingly, they aren't likely to have many successful relationships.

Finally, you can calm down inside. This means not just controlling your outward behavior, but also controlling your internal responses, taking steps to lower your heart rate, calm yourself down, and let the feelings subside.

As Dr. Spiel Berger notes, "When hone of these three techniques work, that's when someone—or something—is going to get hurt."

Anger Management

The goal of anger management is to reduce both your emotional feelings and the physiological arousal that anger causes. You can't get rid of, or avoid, the things or the people that enrage you, nor can you change them, but you can learn to control your reactions.

Are You Too Angry ?

There are psychological tests that measure the intensity of angry Feelings, how prone to anger you are, and how well you handle it. But chances are good that if you do have a problem with anger, you already know it. If you find yourself acting in ways that seem out of control and frightening, you might need help finding better ways to deal with this emotion.

Why Are Some People More Angry Than Others?

According to Jerry Dieffenbachia, PhD, a psychologist who specializes in anger management, some people really are more "hotheaded" than others are; they get angry more easily and more intensely than the average person does. There are also those who don't show their anger in loud spectacular ways but are chronically irritable and grumpy. Easily angered people don't always curse and throw things; sometimes they withdraw socially, sulk, or get physically ill.

People who are easily angered generally have what some psychologists call a low tolerance for frustration, meaning simply that they feel that they should not have to be subjected to frustration, inconvenience, or annoyance. They can't take things in stride, and they're particularly infuriated if the situation seems somehow unjust: for example, being corrected for a minor mistake.

What makes these people this way? A number of things. One cause may be genetic or physiological: There is evidence that some children are born irritable, touchy, and easily angered, and that these signs are present from a very early age. Another may be sociocultural. Anger is often regarded as negative; we're taught that it's all right to express anxiety, depression, or other emotions but not to express anger. As a result, we don't learn how to handle it or channel it constructively.

Research has also found that family background plays a role. Typically, people who are easily angered come from families that are disruptive, chaotic, and not skilled at emotional communications.

Relaxation

Simple relaxation tools, such as deep breathing and relaxing imagery, can help calm down angry feelings. There are books and courses that can teach you relaxation techniques, and once you learn the techniques, you can call upon them in any situation. If you are involved in a relationship where both partners are hot-tempered, it might be a good idea for both of you to learn these techniques.

Some simple steps you can try:

- Breathe deeply, from your diaphragm; breathing from your chest won't relax you. Picture your breath coming up from your "gut."
- Slowly repeat a calm word or phrase such as "relax," "take it easy." Repeat it to yourself while breathing deeply.
- Use imagery; visualize a relaxing experience, from either your memory or your imagination.
- No strenuous, slow *yoga*-like exercises can relax your muscles and make you feel much calmer.

Practice these techniques daily. Learn to use them automatically when you're in a tense situation.

Cognitive Restructuring

Simply put, this means changing the way you think. Angry people tend to curse, swear, or speak in highly colorful terms that reflect their inner thoughts. When you're angry, your thinking can get very exaggerated and overly dramatic. Try replacing these thoughts with more rational ones. For instance, instead of telling yourself, "oh, it's awful, it's terrible, everything's ruined," tell yourself, "it's frustrating, and it's understandable that I'm upset about it, but it's not the end of the world and getting angry is not going to fix it anyhow."

Be careful of words like "never" or "always" when talking about yourself or someone else. "You're always forgetting things" are not just inaccurate, they also serve to make you feel that your anger is justified and that there's no way to solve the problem. They also alienate and humiliate people who might otherwise be willing to work with you on a solution.

Remind yourself that getting angry is not going to fix anything, that it won't make you feel better (and may actually make you feel worse).

Logic defeats anger, because anger, even when it's justified, can quickly become irrational. So use cold hard logic on yourself. Remind yourself that the world is "not out to get you," you're just experiencing some of the rough spots of daily life. Do this each time you feel anger getting the best of you, and it'll help you get a more balanced perspective. Angry people tend to demand things: fairness, appreciation, agreement, and willingness to do things their way. Everyone wants these things, and we are all hurt and disappointed when we don't get them, but angry people demand them, and when their demands aren't met, their disappointment becomes anger. As part of their cognitive restructuring, angry people need to become aware of their demanding nature and translate their expectations into desires. In other words, saying, "I would like" something is healthier than saying, "I demand" or "I must have" something. When you're unable to get what you want, you will experience the normal reactions—frustration, disappointment, hurt—but not anger. Some angry people use this anger as a way to avoid feeling hurt, but. that doesn't mean the hurt goes away.

Problem Solving

Sometimes, our anger and frustration are caused by very real and inescapable problems in our lives. Not all anger is misplaced, and often it's a healthy, natural response to these difficulties. There is also a cultural belief that every problem has a solution, and it adds to our frustration to find out that this isn't always the case. The best attitude to bring to such a situation, then, is not to focus on finding the solution, but rather on how you handle and face the problem.

Make a plan, and check your progress along the way. Resolve to give it your best, but also not to punish yourself if an answer doesn't come right away. If you can approach it with your best intentions and efforts and make a serious attempt to face it head-on, you will be less likely to lose patience and fall into all-or-nothing thinking, even if the problem does not get solved right away.

Better Communication

Angry people tend to jump to—and act on—conclusions, and some of those conclusions can be very inaccurate. The first thing to do if you're in a heated discussion is slow down and think through your responses. Don't say the first thing that comes into your head, but slow down and think carefully about what you want to say. At the same time, listen carefully to what the other person is saying and take your time before answering.

Listen, too, to what is underlying the anger. For instance, you like a certain amount of freedom and personal space, and your "significant other" wants more connection and closeness. If he or she starts complaining about your activities, don't retaliate by painting your partner as a jailer, a warden, or an albatross around your neck.

It's natural to get defensive when you're criticized, but don't fight back. Instead, listen to what's underlying the words: the message that this person might feel neglected and unloved. It may take a lot of patient questioning on your part, and it may require some breathing space, but don't let your anger—or a partner's—let a discussion spin out of control. Keeping your cool can keep the situation from becoming a disastrous one.

Using Humour

"Silly humour" can help defuse rage in a number of ways. For one thing, it can help you get a more balanced perspective. When you get angry and call someone a name or refer to them in some imaginative phrase, stop and picture what that word would literally look like. If you're at work and you think of a coworker as a "dirtbag" or a "single-cell life form," for example, picture a large bag full of dirt (or an amoeba) sitting at your colleague's desk, talking on the phone, going to meetings. Do this whenever a name comes into your head about another person. If you can, draw a picture of what the actual thing might look like. This will take a lot of the edge off your fury; and humor can always be relied on to help unknot a tense situation.

The underlying message of highly angry people, Dr. Deffenbacher says, is "things ought to go my way!" Angry people tend to feel that they are morally right, that any blocking or changing of their plans is an unbearable indignity and that they should NOT have to suffer this way. Maybe other people do, but not them!

When you feel that urge, he suggests, picture yourself as a god or goddess, a supreme ruler, who owns the streets and stores and office space, striding alone and having your way in all situations while others defer to you. The more detail you can get into your imaginary scenes, the more chances you have to realize that maybe you are being unreasonable; you'll also realize how unimportant the things you're angry about really are. There are two cautions; in using humor. First, don't try to just "laugh off" your problems; rather, use humor to help yourself face them more constructively. Second, don't give in to harsh, sarcastic humor; that's just another form of unhealthy anger expression.

What these techniques have in common is a refusal to take yourself too seriously. Anger is a serious emotion, but it's often accompanied by ideas that, if examined, can make you laugh.

Changing Your Environment

Sometimes it's our immediate surroundings that give us cause for irritation and fury. Problems and responsibilities can weigh on you and make you feel angry at the "trap" you seem to have fallen into and all the people and things that form that trap.

Give yourself a break. Make sure you have some "personal time" scheduled for times of the day that you know are particularly stressful. One example is the working mother who has a standing rule that when she comes home from work, for the first 15 minutes "nobody talks to Mom unless the house is on fire." After this brief quiet time, she feels better prepared to handle demands from her kids without blowing up at them.

Some Other Tips for Easing Up on Yourself

Timing: If you and your spouse tend to fight when you discuss things at night—perhaps you're tired, or distracted, or maybe it's just habit—try changing the times when you talk about important matters so these talks don't turn into arguments.

Avoidance: If your child's chaotic room makes you furious every time you walk by it, shut the door. Don't make yourself look at what infuriates you. Don't say, "well, my child should clean up the room so I won't have to be angry!" That's not the point. The point is to keep yourself calm.

Finding alternatives: If your daily commute through traffic leaves you in a state of rage and frustration, give yourself a project—learn or map out a different route, one that's less congested or more scenic. Or find another alternative, such as a bus or commuter train.

Do You Need Counseling?

If you feel that your anger is really out of control, if it is having an impact on your relationships and on important parts of your life, you might consider counseling to learn how to handle it better. A psychologist or other licensed mental health professional can work with you in developing a range of techniques for changing your thinking and your behavior.

When you talk to a prospective therapist, tell her or him that you have problems with anger that you want to work on; and ask about his or her approach to anger management.

Make sure this isn't; only a course of action designed to "put you in touch with your feelings and express them"—that may be precisely what your problem is. With counseling, psychologists say, a highly angry person can move closer to a middle range of anger in about 8 to 10 weeks, depending on the circumstances and the techniques used.

Anger Management Tips

- *Find a safe spot :* Yelling at friends or family members, slamming doors, and breaking crockery doesn't solve any problem and frequently escalates angry situations between people. Yet, sometimes you just need to vent. Finding a safe spot to act our your anger can relieve the majority of your stress, calming you enough to solve the real problem at hand. Go to a basement room and scream your head off! Take an empty jar to your basement and break it, (remember to sweep up when you're done). Stomp on a few aluminum cans. Throw a tennis ball at the garage wall. Buy a punching bag.
- *Breath deep :* Anger often begins when we feel weaker than we really are. Molehills loom like mountains. Taking a few deep breaths calms you, makes you feel stronger both mentally and physically, and can cut those mountains down to size!
- *Count to ten :* Sounds simple, but counting to ten is an anger management tip that has worked for centuries! The Roman poet Horace (65 – 8 BCE) said, "When angry, count ten before you speak; if very angry, one hundred." Counting to ten (or one hundred) helps you to step back from the situation, buys time for you to examine the problem and decide on an effective, rational way to express your anger.
- *Give yourself a break :* It's easier to think when you're calm than when you're agitated. Leave the room, take a walk, 'whistle a happy tune'. Then come back to the problem, examine it, and solve it.

- Look for the sweet spot. Learn to act and not react. Although every cloud doesn't have a silver lining, when life hands you a lemon, you can make lemonade and when you get angry, you can find a positive way to express it!

Anger Management Techniques

One of the greatest detriments of anger is that it makes us feel helpless and out of control. Anger management techniques aren't meant to eliminate your anger. Anger management techniques put you in charge of the situation and teach you how to make your anger work for you.

When we take the attitude that "there's no time like the present" to vent our anger and "let it rip", anger often tears huge holes in the fabric of our lives, dropping us down the rabbit hole with no way up! Anger management techniques help you learn to express your anger in constructive ways and sew up your problems before you find yourself trying to mend fences instead.

Silly mental pictures can help diffuse anger in many situations.

Accentuate the Positive

Your partner or spouse is late again and it's making you mad.as a hatter. Picture yourself at the "Mad Hatter's tea party", the White Rabbit making his entrance "I'm late—I'm always late". Surely, the Cheshire cat's smile is growing in the background as the angry dormouse shrinks back into the teapot! Why? [Because your partner's tardiness just bought you some extra time!

- Use the time to file your nails, read that magazine article you don't have time to read, file your nails, and check your e-mail...

Put your Anger on Hold

Your partner arrives an hour late and full of excuses. You've managed to stay reasonably calm, but you can see your anger rearing its head. Say, "I know White Rabbit. Let's talk about it later and smile! You are still in control of your emotions and the situation; that's what's important. Timing is often critical to keeping anger at bay. Don't discuss issues when you're tired, or the situation has already made you irritable. Do choose a time to find solutions to problems; just make it when you can talk rationally and comfortably—when you can stay in control.

Let Humour Calm you Down

- Ex: Another driver "cuts you off" in traffic. Break it down to the ridiculous. Lean back in your seat and take a deep breath. Breathe a sigh of relief that you at least still have your legs! Picture how silly you must look to other drivers, tooling down the road in your "cut off vehicle. Parallel parking will sure be a breeze now, won't it?

Don't React to Anger-Respond

A major anger management technique is in changing the way you think and learning to respond to anger instead of reacting to it. Reacting to anger is a learned, impulsive behavior that becomes instinctive. Responding to anger allows you to examine various solutions and gives you the opportunity to choose the one that works the best for you.

Take Care of You

- Make personal time each day to reflect on issues and consider solutions to problems.
- Work for balance in your life. Try to leave work problems at work and personal problems at home.
- Although we tend to often separate mind and body, they work together to make each of us into one unique being. Regular exercise, healthy eating, and adequate

sleep are as essential to your emotional health as they are to your physical well-being.

Don't look Back, Move Forward

Yelling, "This blasted machine never works!" doesn't make the machine work. "You're always late!" doesn't change what happened in the past and makes no plans for change in the fuiure, except maybe for a destroyed friendship. When you put the lid on past problems, you free up time now to find solutions for current and future problems—anger management: techniques to secure the lid on that grumpy dormouse.

Anger Management Exercises

Although reaction to anger is often characterized as boiling overdo, exploding, or loosing your cool, intense anger reactions vary from violent physical displays to depression. Along with punching and smashing, angry people also loose control and yell, curse, make sarcastic comments, become depressed, shake, feel nauseous, feel dizzy, get headaches, and cry.

The anger management exercise below will help you find your anger triggers, evaluate, and change your reactions to anger:

1. Think of five things that always make you angry or annoy you. These are anger triggers and they can range from small annoyances to volcanic events. For instance, an anger trigger may be a finger-drumming acquaintance, a neighborhood-barking dog, a driver who cuts you off in traffic, or just the stop-go frustration of rush hour on an Interstate highway.
2. Rate the five triggers from one to five as to how much they irritate you.
3. How do you react to each trigger? Some negative reactions are in the list below:

A. Do you get into physical fights with others?

B. Do you punch, hit, or kick inanimate objects or pets?

Getting physical is never a long-term solution to problems. If either A or B is a common reaction to anger, consider finding help in an anger management class, a support group, or through private counseling.

C. Do you frequently slam doors, sometimes to the point of damaging them?

D. Do you throw, break, or destroy objects to relieve your anger?

E. Do you stomp your feet in anger?

Although none of these solves the problems that made us angry, you can adapt them to help relieve some of the adrenaline that makes anger erupt. Find a safe place and tantrum away! After you're calm again, examine what happened and use anger management strategies and anger management techniques to keep it from happening again.

F. Do you yell until you're hoarse? Do you often say things that you regret later?

G. Do you face confrontation with sarcasm?

H. Do you often say things that you later regret?

If you answered yes to F, G, or H you're probably finding that none solves the problems that stir up your anger. Brainstorm to find better avenues of communication. Then use anger management strategies and anger management techniques to help you resolve your anger triggers.

I. Do you shy away from confrontation? Do you keep your feelings to yourself?

J. Do you brood over the unfairness or hopelessness of situations?

K. Do you say, well talk about it later and never do?

Internalized anger can lead to both physical health problems (such as nausea, dizziness, indigestion) and mental health problems like depression. If your response to I, J, or K was eyes, consider taking an anger management class, some assertiveness training, or finding help through private counseling.

Anger Management for Teens

Now that you're a teen, you probably hear a lot about teen hormones, teen mood swings, and teen problems (as if you weren't living through them)! It's enough to make anyone mad, but here's the thing—teenage anger is a normal part of growing. Besides, anger is a normal emotion for everybody—little kids, teens, and adults. While anger often gets a bad rap, it isn't bad to get angry.

Anger is just another emotion like love, hate, joy, and sorrow. The trick to anger management, like any other emotion, is how you express it. If something makes you happy, depending on what it is and who did it, you might express your happiness with a smile, a hug, or a kiss. Expressing anger is the same. Anger works for you when you choose how to express it. Choosing how to express your anger is anger management.

Anger is a signal that something's not right. It actually can help you get through a dangerous situation or give you courage to stand up for your rights when you've been wronged. The problem with anger is that it's fueled with adrenaline and it's easy to let that rush take control, making you feel overwhelmed, powerless, and out of control.

Many things in life can stir up your anger. You can get angry over a lost game, a cancelled concert, or people (classmates, teachers, parents—even your best friend) may do things that don't "sit right" with you. At times, you've probably even been angry with yourself for wearing the wrong thing, saying the wrong thing, or doing the wrong thing. Even just growing can make you angry. ("I hate being so short, so fat so thin, so tall...!").

Temper Tools

Although anger is a normal, healthy emotion it's also a powerful emotion that can get in the way of what you want. Learning to channel your anger helps you to get from point "A" to point "B" without destroying everything in your path. It takes both time and practice to develop good anger management skills. By the time you're a teen, you have the tools you need to manage your anger. The challenge is learning how to use them to get the best results.

The most valuable tool you have for managing anger is self-control. Fortunately, it's a tool that you've been sharpening for years. Self-control keeps you from telling your Mom that her roast beef is crummy or your best friend that her new bedroom wallpaper looks stupid. It keeps you from cutting class just because you forgot about the test.

Luckily, when you begin to get angry, your body gives you physical signals. You begin to feel warm and flushed, your heart starts to pound, and your skin feels "tight" or tingly. It's time to step back, take a deep breath, and put the self-control in gear.

Using self-control when you're angry can keep you from saying or doing something that makes you look foolish. It can make the difference between stumbling over a chair, kicking it and really hurting your foot or just moving the chair out of your way. It can make the difference between saying or doing something now that you'll need to apologize for later or even worse, something that an apology won't fix.

One way to imprint the benefits of anger management is to look at the ways you react to anger. How do you feel after you've vented your anger? We rarely are rewarded for reacting to anger; instead, we usually end up paying the consequences.

Look at past situations and examine what you could have done differently to arrive at a better outcome. Would a better response to anger have earned you more respect from others or more self-respect? Did your actions result in positive change, negative change, or no change at all?

Managing Anger

1. Tune in to your feelings. Note what makes you angry and why. Don't settle for pat explanations like "It's not fair," Ask yourself why you feel it's not fair, what needs to be done to make it fair, and; what the best way is to bring about that change.
2. Step back and think when you begin to fee! angry. Turn on the self-control. Take a minute to define what's making you angry and what you can do to solve the problem.
3. Practice damage control. Choose the solution that gives you the most benefit with the least damage.
4. Although anger often makes mountains out of mole-hills, sometimes the mountains are really mountains. Some problems are just too big for anyone to handle alone. When that's the case, seek help from a parent, counselor, or other trusted adult to help you find the resolution to your anger.

Consider getting anger management help when:

1. You get into physical fights.
2. You find yourself arguing heatedly and often with no resolution.
3. You can't get over a past situation or occurrence.
4. You're in a bad mood more often than a good one.
5. Your anger makes you want to "get back" at something or someone.
6. Your anger makes you want to hurt someone else or yourself.

Always remember: You can either react to angry feelings (kick that chair) or respond to them. Responding to anger takes practice, but keeping the benefits of anger management in mind makes it a lot easier to practice.

It's not bad to feel angry. When expressed constructively it can increase your self-respect as well as others respect for you. Anger management can be a tool you can use to solve problems and make positive change during tough teenage years and it's a tool that lasts a lifetime!

Anger Management for Children

Anger management clearly needs to be a priority for raising our children.

Research from the Columbia University College of Physicians and Surgeons and the New York State Psychiatric Institute indicates that child behaviour problems are omens of adult partner violence as are severe punishment (abuse) arid childhood exposure to abusive relationships between adults.

Another study, completed in 2000, rated childhood tantrums and irritability for children born in 1970. However, the most remarkable information the study uncovered is that children who had been consistently angry in childhood were more likely to be unsatisfied with life at age 30.

The best anger management strategy for children is for you, as a parent, to be a good role model; to familiarize yourself with anger management tips, strategies, and techniques that both help you to cope with the stresses of modern day living as well as being anger management tools to share with your children.

Experts also suggest that to be most effective, anger management for children needs to be implemented before adolescence. Additionally, when a child learns to control his/her anger m pre-teen years, parents reap the benefit of a calmer environment during the child's adolescence!

Anger Management for Infants?

When my daughter was an infant, she frequently woke in a rage, stiffening her body and screaming uncontrollably. When she could stand, she actually threw herself from her crib. Our pediatrician suggested we put her on a blanket in the middle of the floor in a child-safe place and walk away.

One of the hardest things a parent has to do is walk away from a raging child, but it worked. Within just a few days, the rages stopped and our daughter was safe and happy! Her "floor" blanket became one of her favorite friends, which caused me to wonder if Peanuts' Lines had the same problem as an infant.

Anger management tips : Tame your temper controlling your temper isn't always easy. But these effective anger management techniques will help give you the upper hand.

If your outbursts, rages or *bullying* are negatively affecting relationships with family, friends, co-workers and even *complete strangers,* it's time to change the way you express your anger. You can take steps on your own to improve your anger management.

Anger Management Tips

Here are some anger management tips to help get your anger under control:

- Take a "time out." Although it may seem cliche, counting to 10 before reacting, or leaving the situation altogether, really can defuse your temper.
- Do something physically exerting. Physical activity can provide an outlet for your emotions, especially if you're about to erupt. Go for a brisk walk or a run, swim, lift weights or shoot baskets.
- Find ways to calm; and soothe yourself. Practice deep-breathing exercises, visualize a relaxing scene, or repeat a calming word or phrase to yourself, such as "take it easy." You can also listen to music, paint, journal or do *yoga*.
- Once you're calm, express your anger as soon as possible so that you aren't left stewing. If you simply can't express your anger in a controlled manner to the

person who angered you, try talking to a family member, friend, counselor or another trusted person.

- Think carefully before you say anything so that you don't end up saying something you'll regret. Write a script and rehearse it so that you can stick to the issues.
- Work with the person who angered you to identify solutions to the situation.
- Use "I" statements when describing the problem to avoid criticizing or placing blame. For instance, say "I'm upset you didn't help with the housework this evening," instead of, "You should have helped with the housework." To do otherwise will likely upset the other person and escalate tensions.
- Don't hold a grudge. Forgive the other person. It's unrealistic to expect everyone to behave exactly as you want.
- Use humor to release tensions, such as imagining yourself or the other person in silly situations. Don't use sarcasm, though—it's just another form of unhealthy expression.
- Keep an anger log to identify the kinds of situations that set you off and to monitor your reactions.
- Practice relaxation skills. Learning skills to relax and de-stress can also help control your temper when it may flare up.

Sticking with Anger Management Skills

It may take some time and intense effort to put these tips into practice when you're facing situations that typically send you into a rage. In the heat of the moment, it can be hard to remember your coping strategies.

You may need to keep something with you that serves as a reminder to step back from the situation and get your anger under control. For instance, you may want to keep a small, smooth stone in your pocket or a scrap of paper with your tips written down. With due diligence, these anger management techniques will come more naturally and you'll no longer need such reminders.

Getting Professional Anger Management Help

You can practice many of these anger management strategies on your own. But if your anger seems out of control, is hurting your relationships or has escalated into violence, you may benefit from seeing a psychotherapist or an anger management professional. Role playing in controlled situations, such as anger management classes, can help you practice your techniques.

Anger Management Tips

There are three kinds of situation in which we need to learn to be patient:

- When we are experiencing suffering* hardship, or disappointment
- When we are practising Dharma
- When we are harmed or criticized by others

Correspondingly, there are three Types of Patience

- The patience of voluntarily accepting suffering,
- The patience of definitely thinking about Dharma,
- The patience of not retaliating.

These three types of patience do not come easily, and may seem somewhat strange when we first read about them. However, once we understand them clearly and put them into practice sincerely and skilfully, they will liberate our mind from one of its most obsessive delusions and bring great peace and joy. It is therefore worthwhile to persevere in these practices even if initially they may seem unusual or even unnatural.

An in-depth explanation of these 3 types of patience can be found in Venerable Geshe Keisang Gyatso's How to Solve Our Human Problems.

Anger Management Techniques—The Roots of Anger

You can learn anger management techniques, regardless of the cause of your anger. Admitting the fact that your anger is out-of-control is essential to tackling the problem. Excessive anger can be caused by health problems, family issues, drug or alcohol abuse, financial despair, extreme fear or stress, and spiritual void. Uncontrolled anger results in added troubles to your life. But you *can* control your anger! Controlling your *anger Is a choice you can make!*

Anger Management Techniques—Effects

Uncontrolled anger has long-term emotional and physical effects on our body:

- *Physical effects:* Anger causes injury, increased adrenalin surges, high blood pressure, and increased heart rate; possibly producing stroke, and heart attacks.
- *Emotional effects:* Anger creates intense guilt, feelings of failure, depression, constant agitation, violent rage, and possibly suicide.

Anger Management Techniques—Choices

Anger is a very strong emotion. Uncontrolled anger is a life-long pattern. It is not easy to overcome anger; it requires determined commitment. It requires honesty, courage, and tremendous inner strength, ft also requires help from others. To overcome anger, these steps are important:

- *Consciously determine to be calm :* Don't react, think! Remember your goals and respond appropriately. Choose to remain calm!
- *Communicate :* When someone upsets you, tell them. Calmly talk to them about how you feel about their words or actions. Learn to express yourself better—- clear and composed. Choose to!
- *Remove yourself from the scene until you can respond without anger*. Your success will not happen overnight.

Take it one step at a time, one day at a time. Remember to relax. Relaxation exercises or music can be helpful. Keep in mind you can reach out to someone you trust for help. Choose to!

- *Frequently take time for yourself :* Do something you enjoy like walking in the park, swimming, reading the Bible, or seeing a feel-good movie. Do something nice for someone you admire. It's okay to feel good about yourself. Choose to!
- *Look for the positives :* Don't dwell on the negatives. "Don't sweat the small stuff." Learn to be forgiving. This is difficult, but we need to start by learning to forgive ourselves!

Anger Management Techniques—Gaining Perfect Peace

A person having difficulty controlling his anger is not a bad person. Anger against 'wrong' is not sin! It is no disgrace to admit we have a problem and seek outside help. Peace, and the solution to life's problems, can only be found by turning to God. There are many Bible verses that deal specifically with anger and its implications. You need to pray for strength and self control to enjoy a life of contentment and joy. You also need to pray to God to remove the darkness of anger controlling you. Choose it! "You (God) will keep in perfect peace all who trust in you, whose thoughts are fixed on you.

CHAPTER 5

Anger Management Strategy

Dr. K. Sri Ramulu*

Everyone at one point or another has had been angry. Learning how to deal with anger is vital in having healthy lifestyle:

- Anger Management Tips.
- Anger Management Strategies.
- Anger Management Techniques.
- Anger Management Exercises.
- Anger Management for Teens.
- Anger Management in Children.

"Anybody can become angry—that is easy; but to be angry with the right person, and to the right degree, and at the right time, and for the right purpose, and in the right way— that is not within everybody's power and is not easy." **–Aristotle**

What is Anger?

Anger is a natural emotion. It's nature's way of telling us that something in our lives has gone haywire. Anger occurs as a defensive response to a perceived attack or threat to our well-being. In addition to psychological changes, like any

* Department of Commerce, Government Arts College, Srikakulam (A.P.).

emotion, anger is accompanied by physiological changes. When you get angry your adrenaline flows, your heart rate increases, and your blood pressure escalates. The phrase, "I'm so mad my blood is boiling" isn't that far from true when you fly into a rage!

Sometimes just our perception of a situation causes anger to ignite and sometimes the threat may be real. Whatever the case, anger isn't the problem. The problem with anger is that many of us don't learn to manage anger effectively. In fact, one out of five Americans has an anger management problem.

Domestic abuse, road rage, workplace violence, divorce, and addictions are a few of the external examples of the results of poor anger management. Moreover, anger can lead to physical problems when not properly managed. Long-term anger has been linked to chronic headaches, sleep disorders, digestive problems, high blood pressure, and even heart attack.

Yet, when you learn how to manage anger, it can be an accelerant towards positive change instead of a negative propeller towards disaster.

The Sequence of Anger

Anger is usually "triggered" by an occurrence, like stubbing your toe on an inanimate object or by something that someone says. Next, you think something like "what did I do to deserve that". However, at this point, emotion takes over your mind and the "pain" of the situation leads you to believe the answer to your question is "Nothing. I didn't deserve that at all!" Feelings of hurt and betrayal further try to override logic and you're ready to act on your anger by either suppressing it or expressing it.

Suppressing your anger may lead you to believe you have it under control. However, suppressing anger doesn't solve your problem and is a dangerous type of anger management. Suppressed anger stays with you over time and can lead to mental health problems like depression, and physical problems like "stress" headaches and high blood pressure. Additionally, continually suppressing your anger can curtail your ability to act in the face of a real threat to your well-being.

Anger needs to be expressed. Yet, aggressive displays of anger can result in violent eruptions that further hurt you socially, mentally, and physically. The goal of anger management is to help you find healthy ways to express your anger and resolve the problems that ignite it. The first step in anger management is learning to define the problem and face it head on!

Anger Management Tips

- *Find a safe spot.* Yelling at friends or family members, slamming doors, and breaking crockery doesn't solve any problem and frequently escalates angry situations between people. Yet, sometimes you just need to vent. Finding a safe spot to act our your anger can relieve the majority of your stress., calming you enough to solve the real problem at hand. Go to a basement room and scream your head off! Take an empty jar to your basement and break it, (remember to sweep up when you're done). Stomp on a few aluminum cans. Throw a tennis ball at the garage wall. Buy a punching bag.
- *Breath Deep.* Anger often begins when we feel weaker than we really are. Molehills loom like mountains. Taking a few deep breaths calms you, makes you feel stronger both mentally and physically, and can cut those mountains down to size!
- *Count to ten.* Sounds simple, but counting to ten is an anger management tip that has worked for centuries! The Roman poet Horace (65 - 8 BCE) said, "When angry, count ten before you speak; if very angry, one

hundred." Counting to ten (or one hundred) helps you to step back from the situation, buys time for you to examine the problem and decide on an effective, rational way to express your anger.

- *Giveyourself a break.* It's easier to think when you're calm than when you're agitated. Leave the room, take a walk, 'whistle a happy tune'. Then come back to the problem, examine it, and solve it.
- *Look for the sweet spot.* Learn to act and not react. Although every cloud doesn't have a silver lining, when life hands you a lamon, you can make lemonade and when you get angry, you can find a positive way to express it!

Anger Management Strategies

'While anger management tips can help you keep from blowing up, the best anger management strategy is to begin anger management when you're not inflated!

Most experts agree that in order to learn long-term anger management techniques, you first need to recognize the "triggers" that set off your anger. But, what do you do if you're angry most of the time?

An excellent beginning anger management strategy is a small change in your environment. Even a 15-20 minutes environment change, can make a big change in your perspective.

Changing Your Environment

1. If you usually spend your day indoors, make a point to spend some personal time outdoors. Putter in your yard or take a walk. The fresh air will do you good, both physically and mentally.

   If you work mostly outdoors, spend some personal, private time indoors. Go home, put your feet up and relax.

2. If you spend the day in physical labor, give yourself a "quiet time". Sit on a park bench and watch the world go by or sit in your favorite chair and let your tired muscles relax.

   If you spend most of your day ina sit-down job, get those lethargic muscles moving! After work, take some time to walk, run, exercise to feel a surge of renewed energy in both mind and body!

3. If you spend your day in noise, make sure your "quiet time" is quiet. Give yourself a chance to calm down and clear the chaos from your thoughts.

   If you spend your day where the silence is deafening, go home and pump up the volume! Listen to the radio, play a CD, watch an half-hour of television. Get your mind off your problems!

Learn to Recognize Your Anger Activators

When you're reasonably calm, take a few minutes to examine recent times when your anger flared. Jot them down. Don't relive each; just look for what triggered your anger—your anger activators. What started you simmering and when did you boil over? What effect did your temper flares have on those around you and most importantly, you? What resulted from your anger? Let this be the beginning of your anger log or anger diary.

Each day, "log" occurrences of your anger and their triggers. You'll likely find that many of the 'same things are making you see red everyday.

For instance, a lot of folks start each day confronted by the harsh, irritating beeping of an alarm clock. If you're one of them, consider changing its tune. Set a clock radio to music instead of alarm or purchase an alarm that starts with a quiet pulse and slowly increases in intensity.

The Serenity Prayer

You may have heard the platitude, "You're either part of the problem or part of the solution." However, to paraphrase Abe Lincoln:

"You can solve all of the problems some of the time and some of the problems all of the time, but you can't solve all of the problems all of the time."

For instance, when you experience the loss of a family member, the anger you may feel is a natural part of grieving. No matter what you do, you can't solve the problem, but you can learn to control and resolve your anger.

"God grant me the Serenity to accept the things I cannot change. The Courage to change the things we can, And the Wisdom to know the difference."

For decades, Alcoholics Anonymous and other 12-step programmes have used the Serenity Prayer to help their members cope with their problems. Even if you don't believe in a higher power, you can still 'use this simple message as an anger management strategy to help control your anger'.

If anger is affecting your relationships, your work, or your health, consider seeking help. An anger management group, class or private counseling may be your best anger management strategy. Any of these can help you develop an anger management programme based on proven anger management techniques.

Anger Management Techniques

One of the greatest detriments of anger is that it makes us feel helpless and out of control. Anger management techniques aren't meant to eliminate your anger. Anger management techniques put you in charge of the situation and teach you how to make your anger work for you.

When we take the attitude that "there's no time like the present" to vent our anger and "let it rip", anger often tears huge holes in the fabric of our lives, dropping us down the rabbit hole with no way up! Anger management techniques help you learn to express your anger in constructive ways and sew up your problems before you find'yourself trying to mend fences instead.

Silly mental pictures can help diffuse anger in many situations.

Accentuate the Positive

Your partner or spouse is late again and it's making you mad as a hatter. Picture yourself at the "Mad Hatter's tea party", the White Rabbit making his entrance "I'm late - I'm always late". Surely, the Cheshire cat's smile is growing in the background as the angry dormouse shrinks back into the teapot! Why? Because your partner's tardiness just bought you some extra time!

- Use the time to file your nails, read that magazine article you don't have time to read, file your nails, check your e-mail...

Put your Anger on Hold

Your partner arrives an hour late and full of excuses. You've managed to stay reasonably calm, but you can see your anger rearing its head. Say, "I know White Rabbit. Let's talk about it later and smile! You are still in control of your emotions and the situation; that's what's important. Timing is often critical to keeping anger at bay. Don't discuss issues when you're tired, or the situation has already made you irritable. Do choose a time to find solutions to problems; just make it when you can talk rationally and comfortably -when you can stay in control.

Let Humor Calm You Down

- Ex: Another driver "cuts you off" in traffic. Break it down to the ridiculous. Lean back in your seat and take a deep breath. Breathe a sigh of relief that you at least still have your legs! Picture how silly you must look to other drivers, tooling down the road in your "cut off" vehicle. Parallel parking will sure be a breeze now, won't it?

Don't React to Anger-respond

A major anger management technique is in changing the way you think and learning to respond to anger instead of reacting to it. Reacting to anger is a learned, impulsive behavior that becomes instinctive. Responding to anger allows you to examine various solutions and gives you the opportunity to choose the one that works the best for you.

Take Care of You

- Make personal time each day to reflect on issues and consider solutions to problems.
- Work for balance in your life. Try to leave work problems at work and personal problems at home.
- Although we tend to often separate mind and body, they work together to make each of us into one unique being. Regular exercise, healthy eating, and adequate sleep are as essential to your emotional health as they are to your physical well-being.

Don't Look Back, Move Forward

Yelling, "This blasted machine never works!" doesn't make the machine work. "You're always late!" doesn't change what happened in the past and makes no plans for change in the future, except maybe for a destroyed friendship. When you put the lid on past problems, you free up time now to find solutions for current and future problems—anger management techniques to secure the lid on that grumpy dormouse!

Anger Management Exercises

Although reaction to anger is often characterized as "boiling over", "exploding", or "losing your cool", intense anger reactions vary from violent physical displays to depression. Along with punching and smashing, angry people also "lose control" and yell, curse, make sarcastic comments, become depressed, shake, feel nauseous, feel dizzy, get headaches, and cry.

The anger management exercise below will help you find your anger triggers, evaluate, and change your reactions to anger.

1. Think of five things that always make you angry or annoy you. These are anger triggers and they can range from small annoyances to volcanic events. For instance, an anger trigger may be a finger-drumming acquaintance, a neighborhood barking dog, a driver who cuts you off in traffic, or just the stop-go frustration of rush hour on an Interstate highway.
2. Rate the five triggers from one to five as to how much they irritate you.
3. How do you react to each trigger? Some negative reactions are in the list below:

A. Do you get into physical fights with others?

B. Do you punch, hit, or kick inanimate objects or pets?

Getting physical is never a long-term solution to problems. If either A or B is a common reaction to anger, consider finding help in an anger management class, a support group, or through private counseling.

C. Do you frequently slam doors, sometimes to the point of damaging them?

D. Do you throw, break, or destroy objects to relieve your anger?

E. Do you stomp your feet in anger?

Although none of these solves the problems that made us angry, you can adapt them to help relieve some of the adrenaline that makes anger erupt. Find a safe place and tantrum away! After you're calm again, examine what happened and use anger management strategies and anger management techniques to keep it from happening again.

F. Do you yell until you're hoarse? Do you often say things that you regret later?

G. Do you face confrontation with sarcasm?

H. Do you often say things that you later regret?

If you answered yes to F, G, or H you're probably finding that none solves the problems that stir up your anger. Brainstorm to find better avenues of communication. Then use anger management strategies and anger management techniques to help you resolve your anger triggers.

I. Do you shy away from confrontation? Do you keep your feelings to yourself?

J. Do you brood over the unfairness or hopelessness of situations?

K. Do you say, "We'll talk about it later" and never do?

Internalized anger ca'n lead to both physical health problems (such as nausea, dizziness, indigestion) and mental health problems like depression. If your response to I, J, or K was "yes", consider taking an anger management class, some assertiveness training, or finding help through private counseling.

Anger Management for Teens

Now that you're a teen, you probably hear a lot about teen hormones, teen mood swings, and teen problems (as if you weren't living through them)! It's enough to make anyone mad, but here's the thing—teenage anger is a normal part of growing. Besides, anger is a normal emotion for everybody—little kids, teens, and adults. While anger often gets a bad rap, it isn't bad to get angry.

Anger is just another emotion like love, hate, joy, and sorrow. The trick to anger management, like any other emotion, is how you express it. If something makes you happy, depending on what it is and who did it, you might express your happiness with a smile, a hug, or a kiss. Expressing anger is the same, Anger works for you when you choose how to express it. Choosing how to express your anger is anger management.

Anger is a signal that something's not right. It actually can help you get through a dangerous situation or give you courage to stand up for your rights when you've been wronged. The problem with anger is that it's fueled with adrenaline and it's easy to let that rush take control, making you feel overwhelmed, powerless, and out of control.

Many things in life can stir up your anger. You can get angry over a lost game, a cancelled concert, or people (classmates, teachers, parents-even your best friend) may do things that don't "sit right" with you. At times, you've probably even been angry with yourself for wearing the wrong thing, saying the wrong thing, or doing the wrong thing. Even just growing can make you angry. ("I hate being so short, so fat so thin, so tall...!")

Temper Tools

Although anger is a normal, healthy emotion it's also a powerful emotion that can get in the way of what you want. Learning to channel your anger helps you to get from point "A" to point "B" without destroying everything in your path. It takes both time and practice to develop good anger management skills. By the time you're a teen, you have the tools you need to manage your anger. The challenge is learning how to use them to get the best results.

The most valuable tool you have for managing anger is self-control. Fortunately, it's a tool that you've been sharpening for years. Self-control keeps you from telling your Mom that her roast beef is crummy or your best friend that her new bedroom wallpaper looks stupid. It keeps you from cutting class just because you forgot about the test.

Luckily, when you begin to get angry, your body gives you physical signals. You begin to feel warm and flushed, your heart starts to pound, and your skin feels "tight" or tingly. It's time to step back, take a deep breath, and put the self-control in gear.

Using self-control when you're angry can keep you from saying or doing something that makes you look foolish. It can make the difference between stumbling over a chair, kicking it and really hurting your foot or just moving the chair out of your way. It can make the difference between saying or doing something now that you'll need to apologize for later or even worse, something that an apology won't fix.

One way to imprint the benefits of anger management is to look at the ways you react to anger. How do you feel after you've vented your anger? We rarely are rewarded for reacting to anger; instead, we usually end up paying the consequences.

Look at past situations and examine what you could have done differently to arrive at a better outcome. Would a better response to anger have earned you more respect from others or more self-respect? Did your actions result in positive change, negative change, or no change at all?

Managing Anger

1. *Tune into your feelings.* Note what makes you angry and why. Don't settle for pat explanations like "It's not fair." Ask yourself why you feel it's not fair, what needs to be done to make it fair, and what the best way is to bring about that change.
2. *Step back and think when you begin to feel angry.* Turn on the self-control. Take a minute to define what's making you angry and what you can do to solve the problem.

3. *Practice damage control.* Choose the solution that gives you the most benefit with the least damage.
4. *Although anger often makes mountains out of* molehills, sometimes the mountains are really mountains. Some problems are just too big for anyone to handle alone. When that's the cat;e, seek help from a parent, counselor, or other trusted adult to help you find the resolution to your anger.

Consider getting anger management help when:

1. You get into physical fights.
2. You find yourself arguing heatedly and often with no resolution.
3. You can't get over a past situation or occurrence.
4. You're in a bad mood more often than a good one.
5. Your anger makes you want to "get back" at something or someone.
6. Your anger makes you want to hurt someone else or yourself.

Always remember: You can either react to angry feelings (kick that chair) or respond to them. Responding to anger takes practice, but keeping the benefits of anger management in mind makes it a lot easier to practice.

It's not bad to feel angry. When expressed constructively it can increase your self-respect as well as others respect for you. Anger management can be a tool you can use to solve problems and make positive change during tough teenage years and it's a tool that lasts a lifetime!

Anger Management for Children

Anger management clearly needs to be a priority for raising our children.

Research from the Columbia University College of Physicians and Surgeons and the New York State Psychiatric Institute indicates that child behavior problems are omens of adult partner violence as are severe punishment (abuse) and childhood exposure to abusive relationships between adults.

Another study, completed in 2000, rated childhood tantrums and irritability for children born in 1970. However, the most remarkable information the study uncovered is that children who had been consistently angry in childhoo.d were more likely to be unsatisfied with life at age 30.

The best anger management strategy for children is for you, as a parent, to be a good role model; to familiarize yourself with anger management tips, strategies, and techniques that both help you to cope with the stresses of modern day living as well as being anger management tools to share with your children.

Experts also suggest that to be most effective, anger management for children needs to be implemented before adolescence. Additionally, when a child learns to control his/her anger in pre-teen years, parents reap the benefit of a calmer environment during the child's adolescence!

Anger Management for Infants?

When my daughter was an infant, she frequently woke in a rage, stiffening her body and screaming uncontrollably. When she could stand, she actually threw herself from her crib. Our pediatrician suggested we put her on a blanket in the middle of the floor in a child-safe place and walk away.

One of the hardest things a parent has to do is walk away from a raging child, but it worked. Within just a few days, the rages stopped and our daughter was safe and happy! Her "floor" blanket became one of her favorite friends, which caused me to wonder if Peanuts' Linus had the same problem as an infant.

Unconditional Love—An Exquisite Anger Management Strategy for Children

A father in a supermarket displayed a beautiful expressions of unconditional love that taught bystanders a valuable lesson in anger management for children. His pre-school daughter fell to the floor kicking and screaming in every parent's nightmare, a full-blown in-store temper tantrum. The man scooped the child into his arms and held her to his chest, his strong arms crossed over her small frame as she continued to flail violently against him. He didn't say a word; he just held her close and in moments, the child was at peace. The strength of her father's love alone seemed to calm her.

Helping Children Learn Anger Management

It's important for parents to remember that their children spend just as much time learning about themselves as they do learning about the world around them. Although children need to know that anger is a natural, healthy emotion, they also need to learn that like other emotions-love, sadness, joy-anger needs to be expressed appropriately.

The steps in helping your children learn to manage their anger are the same as the steps for adults. Give them anger management tips for soothing their anger, help them find strategies to stay calm, and teach them techniques for constructively expressing their anger.

The first step in anger management for children is to help your children understand when anger begins. Alert them to the physical symptoms of mounting anger.

- Anger makes you breathe faster.
- Anger makes your face turn red.
- Anger makes your muscles tense and your skin feel tight.

Anger Management Tips for Children

1. Help children calm down and refocus. Take a deep breath and count to ten. If you're still angry, count further or count backwards from 10 to one.
2. Give them alternatives to anger.
    - If a school assignment is too hard, don't get angry; get help from a parent or teacher.

3. Sometimes children can't put their anger into words. Give them some crayons and let them put it on paper. Draw a picture of why you're angry (or a picture of anger).
4. Work off your child's anger:
   - Treat your child to a pillow fight
   - Buy them a punch doll
   - Take them for a walk or bike ride (Don't let angry children ride through the streets alone!).
5. Reward your child with your attention when they control their anger. Go outside and run around the house five times fast. We'll talk when you come back in!

Finally, tell your child that everyone (even you) gets angry. Part of being a good role model is letting your children know that you are susceptible to anger, too. Let your child know about a time when you were angry and anger management helped you successfully resolve the problem in a positive way.

Anger Management Techniques

Anger is one of the most common and destructive delusions, and it afflicts our mind almost every day. To solve the problem of anger we first need to recognize the anger within our mind, acknowledge how it harms both ourself and others, and appreciate the benefits of being patient in the face of difficulties. We then need to apply practical methods in our daily life to reduce our anger and finally to prevent it from arising at all.

What is Anger?

Anger is a deluded mind that focuses on an animate or inanimate object, feels it to be unattractive, exaggerates its bad qualities, and wishes to harm it. For example, when we are angry with our partner, at that moment he or she appears to us as unattractive or unpleasant. We then exaggerate his bad qualities by focusing only on those aspects that irritate us and ignoring all his good qualities and kindness, until we have built up a mental image of an intrinsically faulty person. We then wish to harm him in some way, probably by criticizing or disparaging him.

Because it is based on an exaggeration, anger is an unrealistic mind; the intrinsically faulty person or thing that it focuses on does not in fact exist. Moreover, as we shall see, anger is also an extremely destructive mind that serves no useful purpose whatsoever. Having understood the nature and disadvantages of anger, we then need to watch our mind carefully at all times in order to recognize it whenever it begins to arise.

This explanation of how to overcome our anger through practising patience is based on Guide to the Bodhisattva's *Way of Life,* the famous poem by the great Buddhist Master Shantideva. Though composed over a thousand years ago, this is one of the clearest and most powerful explanations of the subject ever written, and is just as relevant today as it was then.

The Faults of Anger

There is nothing more destructive than anger. It destroys our peace and happiness in this life, and impels us to engage in negative actions that lead to untold suffering in future lives. It blocks our spiritual progress and prevents us from accomplishing any spiritual goals we have set ourself - from merely improving our mind, up to full enlightenment. The opponent to anger is patient acceptance, and if we are seriously interested in progressing along the spiritual path there is no practice more important than this.

Anger is by nature a painful state of mind. Whenever we develop anger, our inner peace immediately disappears and even our body becomes tense and uncomfortable. We are so restless that we find it nearly impossible to fall asleep, and whatever sleep we do manage to get is fitful and unrefreshing. It is impossible to enjoy ourself when we are angry, and even the food we eat seems unpalatable. Anger transforms even a normally attractive person into an ugly red-faced demon. We grow more, and more miserable, and, no matter how hard we try, we cannot control our emotions.

Effects of Anger

One of the most harmful effects of anger is that it robs us of our reason and good sense. Wishing to retaliate against those whom we think have harmed us, we expose ourself to great personal danger merely to exact petty revenge. To get our own back for perceived injustices or slights, we are prepared to jeopardize our job, our relationships, and even the well-being of our family and children. When we are angry we lose all freedom of choice, driven here and there by an uncontrollable rage. Sometimes this blind rage is even directed at our loved ones and benefactors. In a fit of anger, forgetting the immeasurable kindness we have received from our friends, family, or Spiritual Teachers, we might strike out against and even kill the ones we hold most dear. It is no wonder that an habitually angry person is soon avoided by all who know him. This unfortunate victim of his own temper is the despair of those who formerly loved him, and eventually finds himself abandoned by everyone.

Identifying Anger

It is very important to identify the actual cause of whatever unhappiness we feel. If we are forever blaming our difficulties on others, this is a sure sign that there are still many problems and faults within our own mind. If we were truly peaceful inside and had our mind under control, difficult people or circumstances would not be able to disturb this peace, and so we would feel no compulsion to blame anyone or regard them as our enemy. To someone who has subdued his or her mind and eradicated the last trace of anger, all beings are friends. A Bodhisattva, for instance, whose sole motivation is to benefit others, has no enemies. Very few people wish to harm someone who is a friend of all the world, and even if someone did harm him or her, the Bodhisattva would not view this person as an enemy. With his mind dwelling in patience, he would remain calm and untroubled, and his love and respect for his assailant would be undiminished*. Such is the power of a well-controlled mind. Therefore, if we really want to be rid of all enemies, all we need to do is uproot our own anger.

What is Repression?

If we are able to recognize a negative train of thought before it develops into full-blown anger, it is not too hard to control. If we can do this, there is no danger of our anger being 'bottled up' and turning into resentment. Controlling anger and repressing anger are two very different things. Repression occurs when anger has developed fully in our mind but we fail to acknowledge its presence. We pretend to ourself and to others that we are not angry—we control the outward expression of anger but not the anger itself. This is very dangerous because the anger continues to seethe below the surface of our mind, gathering in strength until one day it inevitably explodes.

On the other hand, when we control anger we see exactly what is going on in our mind. We acknowledge honestly the angry stirrings in our mind for what they are, realize that allowing them to grow will only result in suffering, and then make a free and conscious decision to respond more constructively. If we do this skilfully, anger does not get a chance to develop properly, and so there is nothing to repress. Once we learn to control and overcome our anger in this way, we shall always find happiness, both in this life and in our future lives. Those who truly wish to be happy, therefore, should make the effort to free their minds from the poison of anger.

Why we get Angry

Anger is a response to feelings of unhappiness, which in turn arise whenever we meet with unpleasant circumstances. Whenever, we are prevented from fulfilling our wishes, or forced into a situation we dislike—in short, whenever we have to put up with something we would rather avoid—our uncontrolled mind reacts by immediately feeling unhappy. This uncomfortable feeling can easily turn into anger, and we become even more disturbed than before.

The other main reason we become unhappy and angry is because we are faced with a situation we do not want or like. Every day we encounter hundreds of situations we do not like, from stubbing our toe or having a disagreement with our partner, to discovering that our house has burnt down or that we have cancer; and our normal reaction to all of these occurrences is to become unhappy and angry. However, try as we might, we cannot prevent unpleasant things happening to us. We cannot promise that for the rest of the day nothing bad will happen to us; we cannot even promise that we shall be alive to see the end of the day. In samsara we are not in control of what happens to us.

Anger and Relationships

Anger is particularly destructive in relationships. When we live in close contact with someone, our personalities, priorities, interests, and ways of doing things frequently clash. Since we spend so much time together, and since we know the other person's shortcomings so well, it is very easy for us to become critical and short-tempered with our partner and to blame him or her for making our life uncomfortable. Unless we make a continuous effort to deal with this anger as it arises, our relationship will suffer. A couple may genuinely love one another, but if they frequently get angry with each other the times when they are happy together will become fewer and further between. Eventually there will come a point when before they have recovered from one row the next has already begun. Like a flower choked by weeds, love cannot survive in such circumstances.

In a close relationship, opportunities to get angry arise many a times a day, so to prevent the build-up of bad feelings we need to deal with anger as soon as it begins to arise in our mind. We clear away the dishes after every meal rather than waiting until the end of the month, because we do not want to live in a dirty house nor be faced with a huge, unpleasant job. In the same way, we need to make the effort to clear away the mess in our mind as soon as it appears, for if we allow it to accumulate it will become more and more difficult to deal with, and will endanger our relationship. We should remember that every opportunity to develop anger is also an opportunity to develop patience. A relationship in which there is a lot of friction and conflict of interests is also an unrivalled opportunity to erode away our self-cherishing and self-grasping, which are the real sources of all our problems. By practising the instructions on patience explained here, we can transform our relationships into opportunities for spiritual growth.

Anger Creates Enemies

It is through our anger and hatred that we transform people into enemies. We generally assume that anger arises when we encounter a disagreeable person, but actually it is the anger already within us that transforms the person we meet into our imagined foe. Someone controlled by their anger lives within a paranoid view of the world, surrounded by enemies of his or her own creation. The false belief that everyone hates him can become so overwhelming that he might even go insane, the victim of his own delusion.

Dealing with Anger

Since it is impossible to fulfil all our desires or to stop unwanted things happening to us, we need to find a different way of relating to frustrated desires and unwanted occurrences. We need to learn patient acceptance.

Patience is a mind that is able to accept, fully and happily, whatever occurs. It is much more than just gritting our teeth and putting up with things. Being patient means to welcome wholeheartedly whatever arises, having given up the idea that things should be other than what they are. It is always possible to be patient; there is no situation so bad that it cannot be accepted patiently, with an open, accommodating, and peaceful heart.

When patience is present in our mind it is impossible for unhappy thoughts to gain a foothold. There are many examples of people who have managed to practise patience even in the most extreme circumstances, such as under torture or in the final ravages of cancer. Although their body was ruined beyond repair, deep down their mind remained at peace. By learning to accept the small difficulties and hardships that arise every day in the course of our lives, gradually our capacity for patient acceptance will increase and we shall come to know for ourself the freedom and joy that true patience brings.

Anger Management

If we practise the patience of voluntarily accepting suffering, we can maintain a peaceful mind even when experiencing suffering and pain. If we maintain this peaceful and positive state of mind through the force of mindfulness, unhappy minds will have no opportunity to arise. On the other hand, if we allow ourself to dwell on unhappy thoughts there will be no way for us to prevent anger from arising. For this reason Geshe Chekhawa said 'Always rely upon a happy mind alone.'

If there is a way to remedy an unpleasant, difficult situation, what point is there in being unhappy? On the other hand, if it is completely impossible to remedy the situation or to fulfil our wishes, there is also no reason to get upset, for how will our becoming unhappy help? This line of reasoning is very useful, for we can apply it to any situation.

Patient acceptance does not necessarily mean that we do not take practical steps to improve our situation. If it is possible to remedy the situation, then of course we should; but to do this we do not need to become unhappy and impatient. For example, when we have a headache there is no contradiction between practising patience and taking a tablet, but until the tablet takes effect we need to accept whatever discomfort we feel with a calm and patient mind. If instead of accepting our present pain we become unhappy and fight against it, we shall just become tense, and as a result it will take longer to get rid of our headache. For as long as we are in samsara we cannot avoid unpleasant, difficult situations and a certain amount of physical discomfort, but by training our mind to look at frustrating situations in a more realistic manner, we can free ourself from a lot of unnecessary mental suffering.

Instead of reacting blindly through the force of emotional habit, we should examine whether it is helpful or realistic to become unhappy in such situations. We do not need to become unhappy just because things do not go our way. Although until now this has indeed been our reaction to difficulties, once we recognize that it does not work we are free to respond in a more realistic and constructive way.

Controlling Anger Benefits of Patience

In reality most of our emotional problems are nothing more than a failure to accept things as they are—in which case it is patient acceptance, rather than attempting to change externals, that is the solution. For example, many of our relationship problems arise because we do not accept our partner as he or she is. In these cases the solution is not to change our partner into what we would like him to be, but to accept him fully as he is. There are many levels of acceptance. Perhaps we already try to tolerate our partner's idiosyncrasies, refrain from criticizing him or her, and go along with his wishes most of the time; but have we in the depths of our heart given up judging him? Are we completely free from resentment and blaming? Is there not still a subtle thought that he ought to be different from the way he is? True patience involves letting go of all these thoughts.

Accepting Others

Once we fully accept other people as they are without the slightest judgement or reservation—as all the enlightened beings accept us—then there is no basis for problems in our relations with others. Problems do not exist outside our mind, so when we stop seeing other people as problems they stop being problems. The person who is a problem to a non-accepting mind does not exist in the calm, clear space of patient acceptance.

Patient acceptance not only helps us, it also helps those with whom we are patient. Being accepted feels very different to being judged. When someone feels judged they automatically become tight and defensive, but when they feel accepted they can relax, and this allows their good qualities to come to the surface. Patience always solves our inner problems, but often it solves problems between people as well.

Anger Management Tips

There are three kinds of situation in which we need to learn to be patient:

- When we are experiencing suffering, hardship, or disappointment
- When we are practising *dharma*
- When we are harmed or criticized by others

Correspondingly, there are three types of patience:

- The patience of voluntarily accepting suffering,
- The patience of definitely thinking about Dharma
- The patience of not retaliating

These three types of patience do not come easily, and may seem somewhat strange when we first read about them.

However, once we understand them clearly and put them into practice sincerely and skilfully, they will liberate our mind from one of its most obsessive delusions and bring great peace and joy. It is, therefore, worthwhile to persevere in these practices even if initially they may seem unusual or even unnatural.

Why We get Angry

Anger is a response to feelings of unhappiness, which in turn arise whenever we meet with unpleasant circumstances. Whenever we are prevented from fulfilling our wishes, or forced into a situation we dislike—in short, whenever we have to put up with something we would rather avoid—our uncontrolled mind reacts by immediately feeling unhappy. This uncomfortable feeling can easily turn into anger and we become even more disturbed than before.

It is a very useful exercise to examine the types of situation in which we get angry. We will probably find that most of our anger arises when our desires are frustrated and we do not get what we want. For example, a man who very much wants to be with his lover will be extremely resentful of anyone or anything that prevents him from doing this. If his lover refuses to see him, or leaves him for someone else, his unhappiness can easily turn into rage. It is essential that we learn new ways of relating to frustrations and disappointments. Since it is unreasonable to expect that we can fulfil all our wants and desires, we must cultivate a more realistic and balanced approach to them.

The other main reason we become unhappy and angry is because we are faced with a situation we do not want or like. Every day we encounter hundreds of situations we do not like, from stubbing our toe or having a disagreement with our partner, to discovering that our house has burned down or that we have cancer. Our normal reaction to all of these occurrences is to become unhappy and angry. However, no matter how much we try we cannot prevent unpleasant things from happening to us. We cannot promise that for the rest of the day nothing bad will happen to us. We cannot even promise that we will be alive to see the end of the day. In samsara we are not in control of what happens to us.

If something can be remedied Why be unhappy about it? And if there is no remedy for it, There is still no point in being unhappy.

If there is a way to remedy an unpleasant, difficult situation, what point is there in being unhappy? On the other hand, if it is completely impossible to remedy the situation or to fulfill our wishes, there is also no reason to get upset, because how will becoming unhappy help? This line of reasoning is very useful because we can apply it to any situation. Patient acceptance does not necessarily mean that we do not take practical steps to improve our situation. If it is possible to remedy the situation, then of course we should, but to do this we do not need to become unhappy and impatient. For example, when we have a headache, there is no contradiction between practicing patience and taking medicine, but until the medicine takes effect we need to accept whatever discomfort we feel with a calm and patient mind. If instead of accepting our present pain we become unhappy and fight against it, we will just become tense, and as a result it will take longer to get rid of our headache. As long as we are in samsara, we cannot avoid unpleasant, difficult situations and a certain amount of physical discomfort, but by training our mind to look at frustrating situations in a more realistic way, we can free ourself from a lot of unnecessary mental suffering.

There are innumerable occasions when it is easy to develop an unhappy mind. When we ourself, our family, or our friends are mistreated, blamed, or are experiencing any kind of misfortune, we normally react by becoming unhappy. We also become unhappy when our relationships are difficult, when we have financial or health problems, when we lose what is important to us, when we are lonely or can never find the time to be alone, when we cannot find work or have too much work, when our dreams and wishes remain unfulfilled or, once fulfilled, leave us feeling hollow and dissatisfied, when we fail or when our success brings with it more stress than we can bear, or when people we dislike are successful—the list is endless. In all these situations our unhappiness can easily lead to a feeling that life or other people are unfair to us, and this depresses us even more.

CHAPTER 6

Anger Management

Sunita Kumari Padhi*
Dr. R.N. Misra**

Introduction

The term *Anger Management* commonly refers to a system of psychological therapeutic techniques and exercises by which someone with excessive or uncontrollable anger can control or reduce the triggers, degrees, and effects of an angered emotional state. In some countries, courses in anger management may be mandated by their legal system. One technique for controlling anger is finding agreement with another person rather than conflict. The use of deep breathing and meditation can be used as a means of relaxation. Other interventions include learning empathy, stress management skills, forgiveness, changing how you speak about yourself or others and improving optimism. As the issue of anger varies from person to person, the treatments are designed to be personal to the individual.

What is Anger

Anger is a natural emotion that every human and many non-human animals experience. Mild forms of human anger may include displeasure, irritation or dislike. When we react

* MPGCMS, SMIT, Berhampur, Orissa.
** Prof. in HRM, PGCMS, SMIT, Berhampur, (BPUT).

to frustration, criticism or a threat, we may become angry - and usually this is a healthy response. Anger may be a secondary response to feeling sad, lonely or frightened.

When anger becomes a full-blown rage our judgement and thinking can become impaired and we are more likely to do and say unreasonable and irrational things. Anger is a deluded mind that focuses on an animate or inanimate object, feels it to be unattractive, exaggerates its bad qualities, and wishes to harm it. For example, when we are angry with our partner, at that moment he or she appears to us as unattractive or unpleasant. We then exaggerate his bad qualities by focusing only on those aspects that irritate us and ignoring all his good qualities and kindness, until we have built up a mental image of an intrinsically faulty person. We then wish to harm him in some way, probably by criticizing or disparaging him. Because it is based on an exaggeration, anger is an unrealistic mind; the intrinsically faulty person or thing that it focuses on does not in fact exist. Moreover, as we shall see, anger is also an extremely destructive mind that serves no useful purpose whatsoever. Having understood the nature and disadvantages of anger, we then need to watch our mind carefully at all times in order to recognize it whenever it begins to arise.

Anger Management Techniques

Anger is one of the most common and destructive delusions, and it afflicts our mind almost every day. To solve the problem of anger we first need to recognize the anger within our mind, acknowledge how it harms both our self and others, and appreciate the benefits of being patient in the face of difficulties. We then need to apply practical methods in our daily life to reduce our anger and finally to prevent it from arising at all.

Identifying Anger

To someone who has subdued his or her mind and eradicated the last trace of anger, all beings are friends.lt is very important to identify the actual cause of whatever unhappiness we feel. If we are forever blaming our difficulties on others, this is a sure sign that there are still many problems and faults within our own mind. If we were truly peaceful inside and had our mind under control, difficult people or circumstances would not be able to disturb this peace, and so we would feel no compulsion to blame anyone or regard them as our enemy. To someone who has subdued his or her mind and eradicated the last trace of anger, all beings are friends. A Bodhisattva, for instance, whose sole motivation is to benefit others, has no enemies. Very few people wish to harm someone who is a friend of all the world, and even if someone did harm him or her, the Bodhisattva would not view this person as an enemy. With his mind dwelling in patience, he would remain calm and untroubled, and his love and respect for his assailant would be undiminished. Such is the power of a well-controlled mind. Therefore, if we really want to be rid of all enemies, all we need to do is uproot our own anger.

Why We get Angry

Anger is a response to feelings of unhappiness, which in turn arise whenever we meet with unpleasant circumstances. Whenever we are prevented from fulfilling our wishes, or forced into a situation we dislike—in short, whenever we have to put up with something we would rather avoid—our uncontrolled mind reacts by immediately feeling unhappy. This uncomfortable feeling can easily turn into anger, and we become even more disturbed than before.

Anger is a response to feelings of unhappiness, which in turn arise whenever we meet with unpleasant circumstances.

The other main reason we become unhappy and angry is because we are faced with a situation we do not want or like. Every day we encounter hundreds of situations we do not like, from stubbing our toe or having a disagreement with our partner, to discovering that our house has burnt down or that we have cancer; and our normal reaction to all of these occurrences is to become unhappy and angry. However, try as we might, we cannot prevent unpleasant things happening to us. We cannot promise that for the rest of the day nothing bad will happen to us; we cannot even promise that we shall be alive to see the end of the day. In samsara we are not in control of what happens to us

Dealing with Anger

Since it is impossible to fulfil all our desires or to stop unwanted things happening to us, we need to find a different way of relating to frustrated desires and unwanted occurrences. We need to learn patient acceptance.

When patience is present in our mind it is impossible for unhappy thoughts to gain a foothold.

Patience is a mind that is able to accept, fully and happily, whatever occurs. It is much more than just gritting our teeth and putting up with things. Being patient means to welcome wholeheartedly whatever arises, having given up the idea that things should be other than what they are. It is always possible to be patient; there is no situation so bad that it cannot be accepted patiently, with an open, accommodating, and peaceful heart. When patience is present in our mind it is impossible for unhappy thoughts to gain a foothold. There are many examples of people who have managed to practice patience even in the most extreme circumstances, such as under torture or in the final ravages of cancer. Although their body was ruined beyond repair, deep down their mind remained at peace. By learning to accept the small difficulties and hardships that arise every day in the course of our lives, gradually our capacity for patient acceptance will increase and we shall come to know for our self the freedom and joy that true patience brings.

Controlling Anger

Many of our relationship problems arise because we do not accept our partner as he or she is. In these cases the solution is to accept him fully as he is. In reality most of our emotional problems are nothing more than a failure to accept things as they are—in which case it is patient acceptance, rather than attempting to change externals, that is the solution. For example, many of our relationship problems arise because we do not accept our partner as he or she is. In these cases the solution is not to change our partner into what we would like him to be, but to accept him fully as he is. There are many levels of acceptance. Perhaps we already try to tolerate our partner's idiosyncrasies, refrain from criticizing him or her, and go along with his wishes most of the time; but have we in the depths of our heart given up judging him? Are we completely free from resentment and blaming? Is there not still a subtle thought that he ought to be different from the way he is? True patience involves letting go of all these thoughts.

The Faults of Anger

There is nothing more destructive than anger. It destroys our peace and happiness in this life, and impels us to engage in negative actions that lead to untold suffering in future lives. It blocks our spiritual progress and prevents us from accomplishing any spiritual goals we have set our self - from merely improving our mind, up to full enlightenment. The opponent to anger is patient acceptance, and if we are seriously interested in progressing along the spiritual path there is no practice more important than this. Whenever we develop anger, our inner peace immediately disappears and even our body becomes tense and uncomfortable.

Anger is by nature a painful state of mind. Whenever we develop anger, our inner peace immediately disappears and even our body becomes tense and uncomfortable. We are so restless that we find it nearly impossible to fall asleep, and whatever sleep we do manage to get is fitful and unrefreshing. It is impossible to enjoy our self when we are angry, and even the food we eat seems unpalatable. Anger transforms even a normally attractive person into an ugly red-faced demon. We grow more and more miserable, and, no matter how hard we try, we cannot control our emotions.

Effects of Anger

One of the most harmful effects of anger is that it robs us of our reason and good sense. Wishing to retaliate against those whom we think have harmed us, we expose our self to great personal danger merely to exact petty revenge. To get our own back for perceived injustices or slights, we are prepared to jeopardize our job, our relationships, and even the well-being of our family and children. When we are angry we lose all freedom of choice, driven here and there by an uncontrollable rage. Sometimes this blind rage is even directed at our loved ones and benefactors.

In a fit of anger, forgetting the immeasurable kindness we have received from our friends, family, or Spiritual Teachers, we might strike out against and even kill the ones we hold most dear. It is no wonder that an habitually angry person is soon avoided by all who know him. This unfortunate victim of his own temper is the despair of those who formerly loved him, and eventually finds himself abandoned by everyone.

Anger Management Tips

Anger that is not managed can seriously damage your relationships, opportunities, and can result into physical violence drastically changing your life. There are various anger management tips that can be followed to prevent anger issues from causing major problems in your life.

- The first anger management tip that you can follow when you feel the emotion of anger is to take a time out.

- The second anger management tip which can help to control the powerful emotion of anger is physical activity.
- The third anger management tip that you can follow when you feel the emotion of anger is taking a minute to calm yourself.
- The fourth anger management tip to follow when you fell the emotion of anger is to use humor. Humor is an excellent method to release aggression.

Anger Management Strategies

Practising different anger management strategies is a great way to gain an accurate perspective and properly deal with your anger issues. There are various anger management strategies that effectively aid in anger management.

- The first anger management strategy that many people with anger problems practice daily is keeping an anger log. Anger logs are journals that you keep and jot down thoughts when you feel angry.
- The second anger management strategy which can be very helpful is to talk yourself down. When you feel yourself getting angry stop and ask yourself several questions.
- The third anger management strategy that many people with anger problems practice is role reversal.

In role reversal you simply put yourself in the other person's place that has angered you.

Anger Management Skills

Anger management skills can be used as excellent tools to control and manage anger. There are six anger management skills that should be mastered to be used to defuse and overcome anger issues.

- The first anger management skill that you should master is the ability to recognize stress. If you can successfully recognize when you are becoming stressed before it develops into anger than you can more easily prevent anger.

- The second management skill is the ability to develop empathy. This skill uses the perspective of others to reduce your anger. The development of empathy also aids in building better relationships with people.
- The third anger management skill that you should master is the ability to respond instead of react. Everyone with anger issues are quick to react instead of to respond. When you respond you think first and effectively communicate your feelings. When you react you are not thinking and simply reacting to what the situation or other person has done or resulted in.
- The fourth anger management skill is the ability to change the current conversation with yourself. Your inner conversation has a major impact on your anger.
- The fifth anger management skill that you should master is the ability to communicate assertively. This skill involves a person practicing effective communication and responding to certain things without getting hostile or angry about it.
- The sixth anger management skill that you should master is the ability to adjust your expectations.

When you do not get something that you expected it can cause the frustration that often leads to anger.

A common skill used in most anger management programs is learning assertive communication techniques. Assertive communication is the appropriate use of expressing feelings and needs without offending or taking away the rights of others. It is typically started with the use of "I" statements followed by a need statement.

Methods of Anger Management

- **Direct :** Such as not beating around the bush, making behavior visible and conspicuous, using body language to indicate feelings clearly and honestly, anger directed at persons concerned.
- **Honourable :** Such as making it apparent that there is some clear moral basis for the anger, being prepared to argue your case, never using manipulation or emotional blackmail, never abusing another person's basic human rights, never unfairly hurting the weak or defenseless, taking responsibility for actions.
- **Focused** : Such as sticking to the issue of concern, not bringing up irrelevant material.
- **Persistent :** Such as repeating the expression of feeling in the argument over and over again, standing your ground, self defense.
- **Courageous :** Such as taking calculated risks, enduring short term discomfort for long term gain, risking displeasure of some people some of the time, taking the lead, not showing fear of other's anger, standing outside the crowd and owning up to differences, using self-protective skills.
- **Passionate :** Such as using full power of the body to show intensity of feeling, being excited and motivated, acting dynamically and energetically, initiating change, showing fervent caring, being fiercely protective, enthusing others.
- **Creative :** Such as thinking quickly, using more wit, spontaneously coming up with new ideas and new views on subject.
- **Forgiveness :** Such as demonstrating a willingness to hear other people's anger and grievances, showing an ability to wipe the slate clean once anger has been expressed.

What to do when You are Angry

There are no fool-proof techniques available for anger management at this stage.This is the most difficult stage to manage because you are the person who is angry and you are the person who is manage yourself. Try one or more of the followings:

1. As soon as you are in control withdraw yourself from the sitiuation to avoid irresponsible or irreversible damage to self, others, relationships, and the environment.
2. When you recognize that you are angry, just stop doing what you have been doing. Walk around or sit calmly for a few minutes.
3. Release the stress (stored due to anger) in a way in which there is at least possible harm to self, others, and the environments.
4. Breathe deeply. Inhale deeply and hold for a second or two. Then exhale deeply. Repeat a few times.
5. Become aware that you are angry just observe yourself.
6. If possible involve in the same creative work that can pacify you.
7. If possible, divert your attention to something else that can relax you: like humour films, calmling musics, Watering your garden, going to beach or park or the like.
8. Postpone the expression of anger again and again.
9. Get into the company of persons you love or who love you and understand you. Speak out of them, if possible.
10. If you have love for children, their presence can pacify you. Even pets can something pacify you.

As for as possible do not swear to yourself or shout like: "I will teach you/him/her a lesson. I will show you/him/her" etc. This will act as a programme and will be stored as negative energy.

Conclusion

Anger management is a practical and down-to-earth programmed that will teach you not only to understand your own anger, but, perhaps just as importantly, how to control the sitituation.... This programme work by addressing the root causes of your fury and help you learn more effective ways to calm down and control your anger. Packed with practical tips, this guide helps you recognize anger triggers, choose effective alternatives, and constructively channel your energy. Anger reactions have been likened to a train running out of control and about to derail. A little anger can motivate us to take action in positive ways. A lot of anger will make us "red with rage." The price for your anger is that you are out of control, you drive away those whom you love the most, and endanger your employment.

CHAPTER 7

Management of Anger : A Tool for Organizational Growth

Prof. S.N. Pathi*
Prof. R.N. Mishra**
Mr. P.C. Sahu***

Introduction

Anger is an emotion. The physical effects of anger include increased heart rate, blood pressure, and levels of adrenaline and noradrenalin. Some view anger as part of the fight or flight brain response to the perceived threat of harm. Anger becomes the predominant feeling behaviourally, cognitively, and physiologically when a person makes the conscious choice to take action to immediately stop the threatening behaviour of another outside force. The English term originally comes from the term angry of Old Norse language. Anger can have many physical and mental consequences.

The external expression of anger can be found in facial expressions, body language, physiological responses, and at times in public acts of aggression. Humans and non-human animals for example make loud sounds, attempt to look physically larger, bare their teeth, and stare. Anger is a behavioural pattern designed to warn aggressors to stop their

* Professor, Business Administration, Berhampur University
** Professor SMIT, Berhampur, Orissa
*** Faculty, CIITM, Berhampur

threatening behaviour. Rarely does a physical altercation occur without the prior expression of anger by at least one of the participants. While most of those who experience anger explain its arousal as a result of "what has happened to them," psychologists point out that an angry person can be very well mistaken because anger causes a loss in self-monitoring capacity and objective observability. In an organization anger plays a significant role for the accomplishment or unproductive of organization as mostly it depends upon the mental state of affairs of the workforce.

Anger management deals with the management of one's anger so that the least possible damage is felt to self, others and the organizational environment. This involves understanding one's anger patterns and dealing with them effectively for successful achievement of organizational goal. The Managers who can manage his own anger effectively can possibly manage the anger of his/or fellow subordinates as well.

How to Manage Anger?

There are different stages how to control or manage the anger. The important three stages are :

Stages of Anger

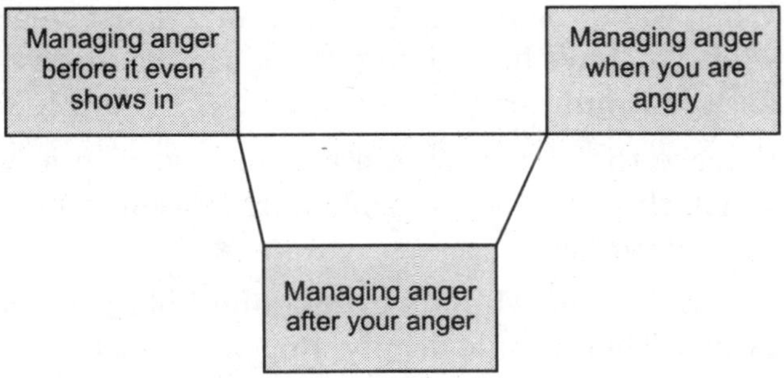

Managing anger before it even shows in

Managing anger when you are angry

Managing anger after your anger

Managing Anger before it ever Appears

Manage your anger before it manages you. This is the *'prevention is better than cure'* approach. This is actually the only effective technique for anger management. This involves two steps:

1. Understanding the root cause of anger in general and of your anger and anger patterns in particular.
2. It also involves having a self-structure that does not pack up stress or that is non-conducive to anger or stress. This is done by continuous practice of some releasing technique such as meditation, relaxation (somatic relaxation like progressive muscular relaxation and psychological relaxation like *sav asana,* autogenic training etc.). And also developing self-confidence, courage etc.

What to Do When You are Angry

There are no fool-proof techniques available for anger management at this stage. This is the most difficult stage to manage because you are the person who is angry and you are the person who is to manage yourself. Try one or more of the following:

- As soon as you are in control withdraw yourself from the situation to avoid irreparable or irreversible damage to self, others, relationships, and the environment.
- When you recognize that you are angry, just stop doing what you have been doing. Walk around or sit calmly for a few minutes.
- Release the stress (stored due to anger) in a way in which there is least possible harm to self, others, and the environment.
- Breathe deeply. Inhale deeply and hold for a second or two. Then exhale deeply. Repeat a few times.
- Become aware that you are angry. Just observe yourself.
- If possible involve in some creative work that can pacify you.

- If possible, divert your attention to something else that can relax you; like humorous films, calming music, watering your garden, going to beach or park or the like.
- Postpone the expression of anger again and again.
- Get into the company of persons you love or who love you and understand you. Speak out to them, if possible.
- If you have love for children, their presence can pacify you.
- Even pets can sometimes pacify you.
- Laugh it out, if you can, by perceiving it in a humorous way.
- Perceive it creatively and constructively and take it as an opportunity to know yourself, your anger patterns and the situation or other people involved.
- As far as possible do not swear to yourself or shout like: 'I will teach you/him/her a lesson. I will show you/him/her' etc. This will act as a programme and will be stored as negative energy.
- Use the Stop Technique.
- Count ten to one repeatedly.

After the Anger Incident

This stage involves two things:

- Analyzing and finding out the root cause of your anger. You will find out that it is one or other kind of fear or attachment.(Attachment also stems from fear).
- Repairing and restoring yourself, others and the environment involved in the anger incident.

Analyzing and Finding Out the Root Cause

You may want or expect others to behave on one way or other and they may do the reverse. This might have made you angry. But why did you expect so? They are free to create their own psychological prisons (= programmes) for themselves. If you have such expectations, come out of these. These expectations, if you look deeply into it are also your own fears in disguise. Attachment to these gives you a security feeling and when they are attacked you become angry. Realize these anxieties and fears. Think of the damages and losses caused to yourself, others and the environment due to your anger. This awareness will lead to an automatic control slowly.

Repairing and Restoring

Repair Yourself

1. Practice relaxation, meditation or any releasing technique so that all ponds up stress energy is either released or dissolved without disturbing yourself, others or the environment.
2. Use humour: read humorous books, watch cartoons or any humorous films etc.

Repair Others and Your Relationships with Them

Apologize if it is appropriate. Do something to recharge your relationship with the persons affected by your temper.

Repair the Environment

If you have disturbed the environment by throwing something, or destroying something, take time to reinstate them as far as possible.

Communication and Conflict

Communication and conflict are related to each other in the sense that communication could lead to conflict as much as conflict could lead to communication. Communication between two individuals could easily lead to conflict especially when there is no middle ground or a point where each party understands and could relate to. On the other hand, conflict can easily lead to communication since this is the only way that two troubled parties could resolve their anger without resorting to physical violence. Communication is very important in dealing with different emotional issues especially anger as it could open up the person for better understanding. Through communication, a person could also express himself which could easily diffuse frustrations, anger, stress and other emotional trouble.

More than Just Talk

But merely talking about your emotions to avoid conflict is not the right way to diffuse emotional problems. As already indicated, proper communication is required so that each party would have a clear understanding. You will most likely end up more frustrated and angry if the communication is not done well. You need to implement assertive communication to be understood. Aside from assertive communication, the physical aspect when talking to another person for an assertive communication should also be considered. Looking straight to the eye will always convey the message clearly. The tone of your voice should also be controlled to prevent the idea that you are conveying an angry message.

Step-by-Step Technique

The following is a recommended strategy on how you can effectively convey your message with understanding. When conveying this message, use first person pronouns (I, we) instead of using 2nd or 3rd person pronouns (you, they) so that you do not sound blaming someone else for your troubles.

The Feeling Stage : The first step in properly conveying your emotion is to tell them how you feel. This should give your listeners a good idea on your current situation.

Pointing to Specific Situation : Inform the person what triggers the said emotions. Although you can be general about the activities, you should be as specific as possible to provide a good example. By being specific, you will also increase understanding since they can easily relate to a specific event.

Reason for Emotions : After stating how you feel towards a specific event, let them know the reason. Emotions are always triggered by events. However, there are underlying reasons why person feels this way. By being honest and clear about the reason, understanding could be achieved.

State What You Need : Close everything by stating what you need to do or what needs to be done by others. At this point, everyone now understands your situation and would be glad to help you with your troubles.

Financial Aspect of Anger

Apart from creating a friendly atmosphere in the workplace, a good reason for managers to control and prevent anger from employees. When conflicts escalate in the office, productivity goes down which means less profits for the company. Although healthy competition could rise, conflicting parties would only think of damaging the other party instead of improving their numbers. It could even get worst when conflict and anger escalates to physical contact among employees. When an employee assaults another employee, the repercussions go beyond simple tension and productivity - someone will be sued, compensation will be provided to those assaulted and anger management program will be implemented on some of the employees. All these happen with corresponding financial responsibility on the part of the company.

Knowing through External Actions

While it is true that work pressure and colleagues could have a major impact on anger issues on the individual, it could be possible that the reason for uncontrollable rage on some employees could come from home. This could be difficult for the managers to know since a proper business relationship has to be established. For that reason, managers have to aid their employees' anger issues based on their external actions. These actions will give managers an idea on how to deal with the situation and see how deep violence could affect work. The assistance offered by managers is aimed to prevent any violent actions escalating at work. When violence happens, it could be said that the managers failed to prevent this type of events from happening because the problem was not addressed as soon as it has started to come out. The external actions are already there so the manager would have noticed these and could have addressed them as soon as possible.

Strategies for Managers

The reason why managers could be blamed for preventing such actions is that they are in a perfect position to implement strategies to prevent workplace violence and anger related problems. There are, in fact, specific strategies for managers to control and prevent anger in workplace. We can place these strategies into two types: the mild and strong strategies. Mild strategy is all about seeking assistance as well as extending emotional help to the employees. Managers can ask company psychologist, psychiatrist and the HR department for evaluation and emotional assistance to their employees. Aside from outside help, managers could also control anger in their employees by implementing "assertive communication" wherein the manager expresses his or her feelings about the situation sternly with a fair reason why these feelings are triggered. Strong strategies are actual managerial actions that will control any confusion in the workplace and prevent anger. There are two things that a manager could do in this strategy. First is to specify the limitation for each employee.

Time Management as the Key

Time management has a direct relation with anger. You can even say that a person who can schedule things and follow them without any problem will most likely be less angry and frustrated. When you can properly manage your time, you will be able to get things done and do not have to deal with the unexpected or, worse, unable to reach the expectations. It goes without saying that anyone who cannot keep up with the expected schedule can only expect challenges since they have to compromise one thing after another.

Family Trouble with Time Management

Time management is often attributed to office and workplace environment. But time management should be observed at home as well. The relationship of work and home will always be there even for those who do not have a family yet. Personal time is very important and highly recommended to everyone. Even robots and machines will experience stress if they are not rested or calibrated from time to time. Humans should also rest and spend time with their family or else stress will increase resulting to decrease in productivity endanger. This can easily happen when you do not have any time management skills.

Getting things Done on Time

Implementing proper time management is very difficult especially if you are inclined to ignore time. But when you are willing to change, things could improve faster than you think it would be. These are the step by step formula on how you can control your time to avoid further emotional problems:

- *Know your limitations :* Time management is all about knowing what you can and cannot do. Always know your limitations and point them out before committing to everything. For example, if you think a specific project will require at least 4 hours, tell your boss about it. Saying "yes" to a 2-hour deadline is very costly.
- *Planning :* Planning things in advance is almost a no-brainer to avoid trouble. But this is a very important step towards better time management. Everything will crumble without proper planning.
- *Back-up plan :* Aside from the time-bound schedule, always have a "Plan B" this will help you prevent any future trouble since you already have a replacement plan in case something bad has happened. This will even serve as a cushion to further trouble since you know that even though things will not work as planned originally, you already have a solution.

- *Rest :* Give yourself time to rest. Weekends or specific time of the day or night should be off-limits to work. This will give you time to recover and think more clearly when you are back at work.

Understand the Importance of ACTS

A - **Aware** of your anger signals

C - **Control** your response

T - **Talk** about the situation in a calm, polite and assertive manner.

S - **Solve** the problem through a mutually agreeable plan of action.

REFERENCES

- Doyle, W., *Anger Management.*
- Israr, Dr. S.M., *Conflict Management*, Aga Khan University, Karachi.
- Les Carter—*Free Yourself from the frustration.*
- Mckay Matthew—*When anger Hurts your relationship.*
- Thomas J. Harbins, Beyond Anger—Da Capo Press.

CHAPTER 8

Managing Anger : The Biggest Challenge for Human Being

Judhisthir Pradhan*
Dr. R.N. Misra*

From the beginning of the civilization of human beings, till date few things are with him irrespective to the time line and the changes in his lifestyle. Anger is one of them. Getting angry is a very common phenomenon for human being. In the modern age almost every body gets angry in different situations and circumstances. Sometimes it gives some good result but, most of the times it results an unhappy or sad end. For example the anger of a soldier towards his enemy provides safegusard to his country and people of his country but at the same time the anger propels a person to commit crime such as murder etc. Similarly, anger of a teacher can motivate a student to achieve the excellence. Hence anger can potentially mobilize psychological resources and boost determination toward correction of wrong behaviours, promotion of social justice, communication of negative sentiment and redress of grievances. It can also facilitate patience. On the other hand, anger can be destructive when it does not find its appropriate outlet in expression. Anger,

---

* MBA, PGCMS, SMDT, Berhampur.
** Prof. MBA, PGCMS, SMDT (B.P.U.T.) Orissa.

in its strong form, impairs one's ability to process information and to exert cognitive control over their behavior. An angry person may lose his/her objectivity, empathy, prudence or thoughtfulness and may cause harm to others. *Oxford's Advanced Dictionary* defines anger as "The strong feeling that you have when something has happened that you think is bad and unfair". This indicates that when the emotions are hurt or when there is no control on emotions, the ultimate result is anger.

Aim and Objectives of the Article

- To find out the kinds of anger expression.
- Analyze the reasons of anger.
- Effect of anger on human being.
- Discuss the solutions.

Kinds of Anger

Many scholars and researchers have classified the anger in various manners. As psychologists define anger is of three forms. They are as follows :

- The first form of anger, named "hasty and sudden anger" by Joseph Butler, an 18th century English bishop, is connected to the impulse for self-preservation. It is shared between humans and non-human animals and occurs when tormented or trapped.
- The second type of anger is named "settled and deliberate" anger and is a reaction to perceived *deliberate* harm or unfair treatment by others. These two forms of anger are *episodic.*
- The third type of anger is however *dispositional* and is related more to character traits than to instincts or cognitions. Irritability, sullenness and churlishness postures are examples of the last form of anger.

As per the symptoms of anger, it can be divided in two categories. They are :

(*a*) Passive anger, and

(*b*) Aggressive anger.

Passive Anger

It can be expressed in the following ways:

- *Secretive behaviour,* such as stockpiling resentments that are expressed behind people's backs, giving the silent treatment or under the breath mutterings, avoiding eye contact, putting people down, gossiping, anonymous complaints, poison pen letters, stealing, and conning.
- *Psychological manipulation,* such as provoking people to aggression and then patronizing them, provoking aggression but staying on the sidelines, emotional blackmail, false tearfulness, feigning illness, sabotaging relationships, using sexual provocation, using a third party to convey negative feelings, withholding money or resources.
- *Self-blame,* such as apologizing too often, being overly critical, inviting criticism.
- *Self-sacrifice,* such as being overly helpful, making do with second best, quietly making long suffering signs but refusing help, or lapping up gratefulness.
- *Ineffectualness,* such as setting yourself and others up for failure, choosing unreliable people to depend on. being accident prone, underachieving, sexual impotence, expressing frustration at insignificant things but ignoring serious ones.
- *Dispassion,* such as giving the cold shoulder or phony smiles, looking unconcerned, sitting on the fence while others sort things out, dampening feelings with substance abuse, overeating, oversleeping, not responding to another's anger, frigidity, indulging in sexual practices that depress spontaneity and make objects of participants, giving inordinate amounts of time to machines, objects or intellectual pursuits, talking of frustrations but showing no feeling.
- *Obsessive behaviour,* such as needing to be clean and tidy, making a habit of constantly checking things,

over-dieting or overeating, demanding that all jobs be done perfectly.

- *Evasiveness,* such as turning your back in a crisis, avoiding conflict, not arguing back, becoming phobic.

Aggressive Anger

The symptoms of aggressive anger are:

- *Threats,* such as frightening people by saying how you could harm them, their property or their prospects, finger pointing, fist shaking, wearing clothes or symbols associated with violent behavior, tailgating, excessively blowing a car horn, slamming doors.
- *Hurtfulness,* such as physical violence, verbal abuse, biased or vulgar jokes, breaking a confidence, using foul language, ignoring people's feelings, willfully discriminating, blaming, punishing people for unwarranted deeds, labeling others.
- *Destructiveness,* such as destroying objects, harming animals, destroying a relationship between two people, reckless driving, substance abuse.
- *Bullying,* such as threatening people directly, persecuting, pushing or shoving, using power to oppress, shouting, using a car to force someone off the road, playing on people's weaknesses.
- *Unjust blaming,* such as accusing other people for your own mistakes, blaming people for your own feelings, making general accusations.
- *Manic behaviour,* such as speaking too fast, walking too fast, working too much and expecting others to tit in. driving too fast, reckless spending.
- *Grandiosity,* such as showing off, expressing mistrust, not delegating, being a sore loser, wanting center stage all the time, not listening, talking over people's heads, expecting kiss and make-up sessions to solve problems.

- *Selfishness,* such as ignoring other's needs, not responding to requests for help, queue-jumping etc.
- *Vengeance,* such as being over-punitive, refusing to forgive and forget, bringing up hurtful memories from the past.
- *Unpredictability,* such as explosive rages over minor frustrations, attacking indiscriminately, dispensing unjust punishment, inflicting harm on others for the sake of it, using alcohol and drugs, illogical arguments.

Causes for Anger

Anger is a normal emotion. We all get angry and need to find ways to manage ourselves when we are angry. The reasons why we get angry are varied. It helps us to find ways to deal with our anger when we understand what is making us angry.

Three reasons people respond with anger when they feel emotionally threatened:

- *Feeling hurt* - when our feelings are hurt it is easier to get in touch with anger at the person who has just emotionally wounded us than to acknowledge the hurt.
- *Feeling betrayed* - the feeling of having been betrayed hits us to the core and again the instinctive response can be one of overwhelming anger at the person who betrayed us.
- *Feeling embarrassed* - responding with anger becomes a way of covering up what one is really feeling.
- Four reasons people respond with anger that are learned.
- *Repeating a pattern* - this is usually a pattern that is learned from the people who have had a significant influence in ones life. Usually it is a parent or other adult from whom one learns how to deal with anger. Unfortunately some people are not good at modeling successful ways of handling oneself when angry.

- *Getting ones way* - Some people have found that they get what they want when they get angry. By getting angry they intimidate the other person and cut off communication.
- *Handling defensiveness* - Responding with anger can be a cover up for feeling defensive. Again it is a learned response to experiencing strong feelings that are deep inside. People who are in the habit of responding with defensive anger are frequently not even aware what they are really feeling. Anger can be a cover-up for many other feelings. It takes courage to look behind the defensiveness.
- *Pent-up rage* - can be for various reasons: having been mistreated, bullied and/or abused; difficulty with impulse control; or a result or drug ,alcohol, or prescription drug abuse. Any one who is struggling with pent-up rage may benefit from a professional assessment. If one does not find successful ways of handling this kind of anger it will adversely affect relationships.

Effect of Anger on Human Being

Anger has both the effect that is positive as well as negative effects on human being.

Positive Effect

In some situations human requires anger to overcome the huddles and win the challenges. Martin Luther had once said" I never work better when I am inspired by anger: when I am angry I can write, pray and preach well, for then my whole temperament is quickened, my understanding sharpen and all mundane vexations and temptation depart" This statement says the importance of anger in the positive and productive ways. Anger is required for the following aspects:

- Anger is a natural response to threats. It allows us to fight and defend ourselves when we are being attacked, however the problem with angry behavior is that, most of the times we use anger when we think we are being attacked without really taking the time to evaluate if we need to feel angry or if we are simply experiencing another emotion such as fear and surprise

- If you are in a dangerous situation, anger could save your life. However if you use anger to handle every situation that arises in your life, anger could ruin your life.
- Anger can also produce powerful changes that can benefit everyone in our society. Anger can make change if it is used appropriately and without aggression and violence.
- How could anger be used positively in your life? Are you in a bad situation in your life and everu dau you make yourself miserable and angry just because you allow yourself to be somewhere? Take that anger and make a move. Let the anger propel you our of a miserable situation into a positive place.

Negative Effect

Anger gives rise to the seven deadly sins.

In AD 590, some years after Evagrius, Pope Gregory I revised this list to form the more common *Seven Deadly Sins,* by folding *sorrow/despair* into *acedia, vainglory into pride,* and adding *extravagance* and *envy,* while removing *fornication* from the list. In the order used by both Pope Gregory and by Dante Alighieri in his epic poem *The Divine Comedy,* the seven deadly sins are as follows:

- *luxuria* (extravagance)
- *gula* (gluttony)
- *avaritia* (avarice/greed)
- *acedia* (acedia/discouragement)
- Ira (wrath)
- *invidia* (envy)
- *superbia* (pride)

luxuria

Luxuria is unrestrained excess. Extravagant behaviour includes the frequent purchase of luxury goods, and forms of debauchery.

In the Romance languages, the cognates *of luxuria* (the Latin name of the sin) evolved to have an exclusively sexual meaning; the Old French cognate was adopted into English as *luxury,* but this lost its sexual meaning by the 14th century.

Gluttony

Derived from the Latin word *gluttire,* meaning to gulp down or swallow, *gluttony* (Latin, *gula*) is the over-indulgence and over-consumption of anything to the point of waste. In the Christian religions, it is considered a sin because of the excessive desire for food, or its withholding from the needy.

Greed

Greed (Latin word *avaritia),* also known as *avarice* or *covetousness,* is, like lust and gluttony, a sin of excess. However, greed (as seen by the church) is applied to a very excessive or rapacious desire and pursuit of wealth, status, and power. St. Thomas Aquinas wrote that greed was "a sin against God, just as all mortal sins, in as much as man condemns things eternal for the sake of temporal things."

Acedia

Acedia (Latin word *acedia)* is the neglect to take care of something-and in this case neglect to do whatever one should do in order to be saved. Dante described acedia as *the failure to love God with all one's heart, all one's mind and all one's soul;* to him it was the *middle sin,* the only one characterized by an absence or insufficiency of love.

Ira (Wrath)

Ira also known as *anger* or "rage", may be described as inordinate and uncontrolled feelings of hatred and anger. These feelings can manifest as vehement denial of the truth, both to others and in the form of self-denial, impatience with the procedure of law, and the desire to seek revenge outside of the workings of the justice system (such as engaging in vigilantism) and generally wishing to do evil or harm to others. The transgressions born of vengeance are among the most serious, including murder, assault, and in extreme cases, genocide. Wrath is the only sin not necessarily associated with selfishness or self-interest (although one can of course be wrathful for selfish reasons, such as jealousy, closely related to the sin of envy). Dante described vengeance as "love of justice perverted to revenge and spite". In its original form, the sin of wrath also encompassed anger pointed internally rather than externally. Thus suicide was deemed as the ultimate, albeit tragic, expression of wrath directed inwardly, a final rejection of God's gifts.

Invidia

Like greed, Invidia (Latin, *invidia*) may be characterized by an insatiable desire; they differ, however, for two main reasons. First, greed is largely associated with material goods, where as envy may apply more generally. Second, those who commit the sin of envy resent that another person has something they perceive themselves as lacking, and wish the other person to be deprived of it. Dante defined this as a desire to deprive other men of theirs." In Dante's Purgatory, the punishment for the envious is to have their eyes sewn shut with wire because they have gained sinful pleasure from seeing others brought low. Aquinas described envy as "sorrow for another's good".

Superbia (Pride)

In almost every list *Pride* (Latin, *superbia),* or *hubris,* is considered the original and most serious of the seven deadly sins, and indeed the ultimate source from which the others arise. It is identified as a desire to be more important or attractive than others, failing to acknowledge the good work of others, and excessive love of self (especially holding self out of proper position toward God). Dante's definition was "love of self-perverted to hatred and contempt for one's neighbour." In Jacob Bidermann's medieval miracle play, *Cenodoxus,* pride is the deadliest of all the sins and leads directly to the damnation of the titulary famed Parisian doctor. In perhaps the best-known example, the story of Lucifer, pride (his desire to compete with God) was what caused his fall from Heaven, and his resultant transformation into Satan. In Dante's *Divine Comedy,* the penitents were forced to walk with stone slabs bearing down on their backs in order to induce feelings of humility.

Along with the above the anger also gives rise to the followings.

Lust

Lust or *lechery,* is usually thought of as excessive thoughts or desires of a sexual nature. Aristotle's criterion was *excessive love of others,* which therefore rendered love and devotion to God as secondary. In Dante's *Purgatorio,* the penitent walks within flames to purge himself of lustful/sexual thoughts and feelings. In Dante's "Inferno" unforgiven souls of the sin of lust are blown about in restless hurricane like winds symbolic of their own lack of self control to their lustful passions in earthly life.

Despair

Despair (Latin, *Tristitia)* describes a feeling of dissatisfaction or discontent, which causes unhappiness with one's current situation, especially involving thoughts of hopelessness. Since unhappiness inherently results from the sin, the sin was sometimes referred to as *sadness.* Since sadness often results in acedia. Pope Gregory's revision of the list subsumed *Despair* into *Acedia.*

Sloth

Gradually, the focus came to be on the consequences of acedia, rather than the cause, and so, by the 17th century, the exact *deadly sin* referred to was believed to be the failure to utilize one's talents and giftsln practice, it came to be closer to *sloth* (Latin, *Socordia)* than acedia. Even in Dante's time there were signs of this change; in his *Purgatorio* he had portrayed the penance for acedia as running continuously at top speed.

The modern view goes further, regarding laziness and indifference as the *sin* at the heart of the matter. Since this contrasts with a more willful failure to, for example, love God and his works, sloth is often seen as being considerably less serious than the other sins, more a sin of omission than of commission.

Religious Perspectives

Catholicism

The Seven Deadly Sins and the Four Last Things, by Hieronymus Bosch(1485). "Anger" is depicted at the bottom in a series of circular images. Below the image is the Latin inscription *Cave Cave Dens Videt* ("Beware, Beware, God is Watching").

Anger in Catholicism is counted as one of the seven deadly sins, although it says in Ephesians 4:26 "be ye angry and sin not". While Medieval Christianity vigorously denounced anger as one of the seven cardinal, or deadly sins, some Christian writers at times regarded the anger caused by injustice as having some value. Saint Basil viewed anger as a "reprehensible temporary madness." Joseph F. Delany in the *Catholic Encyclopedia* (1914) defines anger as "the desire of vengeance" and states that a reasonable vengeance and passion is ethical and praiseworthy. Vengeance is sinful when it exceeds its limits in which case it becomes opposed to justice and charity. For example, "vengeance upon one who has not deserved it, or to a greater extent than it has been deserved, or in conflict with the dispositions of law, or from an improper motive" are all sinful. An unduly vehement vengeance is considered a venial sin unless it seriously goes counter to the love of God or of one's neighbor.

Hinduism

In Hinduism, anger is equated with sorrow as a form of unrequited desire. The objects of anger are perceived as a hindrance to the gratification of the desires of the angry person. Alternatively if one thinks one is superior, the result is grief. Anger is considered to be packed with more evil power than desire. In the *Bhagavad Gita,* Krishna regards greed, anger, and lust as what leads to hell.

Buddhism

Anger in Buddhism is defined here as: "being unable to bear the object, or the intention to cause harm to the object." Anger is seen as aversion with a stronger exaggeration, and is listed as one of the five hindrances. Buddhist monks, such as Dalai Lama, the spiritual leader of Tibetans in exile, sometimes get angry. However, there is a difference; most often a spiritual person is aware of the emotion and the way it can be handled. Thus, in response to the question: "Is any anger acceptable in Buddhism?' the Dalai Lama answered:

"Buddhism in general teaches that anger is a destructive emotion and although anger might have some positive effects in terms of survival or moral outrage, I do not accept that anger of any kind as a virtuous emotion nor aggression as constructive behaviour. The Gautama Buddha has taught that there are three basic kleshas at the root of *samsara* (bondage, illusion) and the vicious cycle of rebirth. These are greed, hatred, and delusion—also translatable as attachment, anger, and ignorance. They bring us confusion and misery rather than peace, happiness, and fulfilment. It is in our own self-interest to purify and transform them." Buddhist scholar and author Geshe Kelsang Gyatso has also explained Buddha's teaching on the spiritual imperative to identify anger and overcome it by transforming difficulties:

When things go wrong in our life and we encounter difficult situations, we tend to regard the situation itself as our problem, but in reality whatever problems we experience come from the side of the mind. If we responded to difficult situations with a positive or peaceful mind they would not be problems for us. Eventually, we might even regard them as challenges or opportunities for growth and development.

Problems arise only if we respond to difficulties with a negative state of mind. Therefore, if we want to be free from problems, we must transform our mind.

Islam

The *Qur'an,* the central religious text of Islam, attributes anger to prophets and believers and Muhammad's enemies. It mentions the anger of Musa (also known as Moses) against his people for worshiping a golden calf; the anger of Yunus (also known as Jonah) God in a moment and his eventual realization of his error and his repentance; God's removal of anger from the hearts of believers and making them merciful after the fighting against Muhammad's enemies is over. In general suppression of anger is deemed a praiseworthy quality and Muhammad is attributed to have said, "power resides not in being able to strike another, but in being able to keep the self under control when anger arises."

Judaism

In Judaism, anger at the sight of wrong done is holy. If the anger kindles into passion, it will become however conducive to strife. According to the Torah: "He that is slow to wrath is of great understanding, but he that is hasty of temper exalteth folly . . . A wrathful man stirrers up strife: he that is slow to anger appeases strife . . . He that is slow to anger is better than the mighty . . . Be not hasty in thy spirit to be angry; for anger rests in the bosom of fools." In the Book of *Genesis*, Jacob condemned the anger that had arisen in his sons Simon and Levi: "Cursed be their anger, for it was fierce; and their wrath, for it was cruel"

Techniques for Managing Anger

Anger is a very common phenomenon. No body in the world can be free from anger. But it must be managed. Followings are few techniques:

- The first step towards managing anger in our personal relationships appropriately is the identification of the mistaken attitudes and convictions that predispose us to being excessively angry in the first place! Once these mistakes have been corrected, we will be less likely to fly off the handle than we were in the past.

- The second step is the identification of those factors from our childhood that prevents us from expressing our anger as appropriately as we otherwise might. These factors include fear, denial, ignorance and so on. These impediments to the effective and appropriate management of our anger towards others can be removed so that our suppressed anger will NOT compound itself inside of us as it has been doing for years.
- The third step is learning the appropriate modes of expressing our "legitimate" anger at others so that we can begin to cope more effectively with anger provoking situations as they arise in our personal relationships. When we are anxious or depressed in our relationships, we are often experiencing the consequences of our suppressed anger. The problem is that we have suppressed our anger so deeply that we succeeded in concealing it from our own selves! All we are left with is the residual evidence of it, our anxiety or our depression. When we are depressed, very often we are also angry at our self without realizing it. Learning to appropriately manage our anger at ourselves is the antidote to much of alcoholism and drug abuse. But the management of our anger does not end in learning these new and more appropriate ways to express it. There remains one last step.
- The fourth step in the Anger Management process is to bind up the wounds that may have been left by the potentially devastating emotional impact of anger. "Anger wounds" left in us against those who have wronged us. If we do not complete this mopping up step, we will cling to the resentment of having been done wrong and will carry the festering residue of our

anger and rage in our hearts forever. One of the most effective means of giving ourselves immediate relief from anger in our personal relationships is to forgive others. With the above *Yoga*, regular exercise and suitable foods are also helpful in managing anger.

Conclusion

Any one can become angry- that is so easy. But become angry with the right person to the right degree at the right time for the right purpose and in the right way- that is no so easy".

REFERENCES

- Albert Ellis and Raymond Tafrate, *How to Control Your Anger Before It Controls You.*
- W. Robert Nay, *Taking Charge of Anger: How to Resolve Conflict, Sustain Relationships, and Express Yourself without Losing Controls.*
- Matthew McKay, Martha Davis and Patrick Fanning, *Thoughts & Feelings: Taking Control of Your Moods and Your Life.*
- Matthew McKay, Peter Rogers, Judith McKay, *When Anger Hurts: Quieting the Storm Within.*

CHAPTER 9

Importance of Anger Management and Its Role

G. Chandrayya*
Dr. D. Tata Rao**

'Anger' is an emotional state that may range in intensity from mild irritation to intense fury and rage. Anger has physical effects including raising the heart rate and blood pressure and the levels of adrenaline and noradrenaline.

Anger is a feeling related to one's perception of having been offended/wronged and a tendency to undo that wrongdoing by retaliation. R. Novaco recognized three modalities of anger: cognitive (appraisals), somatic-affective (tension and agitations) and behavioral (withdrawal and antagonism). Anger may have physical correlates such as increased heart rate, blood pressure, and levels of adrenaline and noradrenaline. Some view anger as part of the fight or flight brain response to the perceived threat of harm. Anger becomes the predominant feeling behaviorally, cognitively, and physiologically when a person makes the conscious choice to take action to immediately stop the threatening behavior of another outside force. The English term originally comes

* Lecturer in Commerce Government College (A) Rajahmundry.
** Senior Faculty Member, Dept. of Commerce Govt. Degree College, Yelemanchili, A.P.

from the term *anger* of Old Norse language. Anger can have many physical and mental consequences.

The external expression of anger can be found in facial expressions, body language, physiological responses, and at times in public acts of aggression. Humans and animals for example make loud sounds, attempt to look physically larger, bare their teeth, and stare. The behaviors associated with anger are designed to warn aggressors to stop their threatening behavior. Rarely does a physical altercation occur without the prior expression of anger by at least one of the participants. While most of those who experience anger explain its arousal as a result of "what has happened to them," psychologists point out that an angry person can be very well mistaken because anger causes a loss in self-monitoring capacity and objective observability.

Modern psychologists view anger as a primary, natural, and mature emotion experienced by all humans at times, and as something that has functional value for survival. Anger can mobilize psychological resources for corrective action. Uncontrolled anger can, however, negatively affect personal or social well-being. While many philosophers and writers have warned against the spontaneous and uncontrolled fits of anger, there has been disagreement over the intrinsic value of anger. Dealing with anger has been addressed in the writings of the earliest philosophers up to modern times. Modern psychologists, in contrast to the earlier writers, have also pointed out the possible harmful effects of suppression of anger. Displays of anger can be used as a manipulation strategy for social influence.

Psychology and Sociology

Anger is viewed as a form of reaction and response that has evolved to enable people to deal with threats. Three types of anger are recognized by psychologists: The first form of anger, named "hasty and sudden anger" by Joseph Butler, an 18th century English bishop, is connected to the impulse for self-preservation. It is shared between humans and non-human animals and occurs when tormented or trapped. The second type of anger is named "settled and deliberate" anger and is a reaction to perceived *deliberate* harm or unfair treatment by others. These two forms of anger are *episodic*. The third type of anger is however *dispositional* and is related more to character traits than to instincts or cognitions. Irritability, sullenness and churlishness postures are examples of the last form of anger.

Anger can potentially mobilize psychological resources and boost determination toward correction of wrong behaviors, promotion of social justice, communication of negative sentiment and redress of grievances. It can also facilitate patience. On the other hand, anger can be destructive when it does not find its appropriate outlet in expression. Anger, in its strong form, impairs one's ability to process information and to exert cognitive control over their behavior. An angry person may lose his/her objectivity, empathy, prudence or thoughtfulness and may cause harm to others. There is a sharp distinction between anger and aggression (verbal or physical, direct or indirect) even though they mutually influence each other. While anger can activate aggression or increase its probability or intensity, it is neither a necessary nor a sufficient condition for aggression.

In Modern Society

The words annoyance and rage are often imagined to be at opposite ends of an emotional continuum: mild irritation and annoyance at the low end and fury or murderous rage at the high end. The two are inextricably linked in the English language with one referring to the other in most dictionary definitions. Recently, Sue Parker Hall has challenged this idea; she conceptualizes anger as a positive, pure and constructive emotion that is always respectful of others; it is only ever used to protect the self on physical, emotional, intellectual and spiritual dimensions in relationships. She argues that anger originates at age 18 months to 3 years to provide the motivation and energy for the individuation developmental stage whereby a child begins to separate from their careers and assert their differences. Anger emerges at the same time as thinking is developing therefore it is always possible to access cognitive abilities and feel anger at the same time.

Parker Hall proposes that it is not anger that is problematic but rage, a different phenomenon entirely; rage is conceptualized as a pre-verbal, pre-cognition, psychological defense mechanism which originates in earliest infancy as a response to the trauma experienced when the infant's environment fails to meet their needs. Rage is construed as an attempt to summon help by an infant who experiences terror and whose very survival feels under threat. The infant cannot manage the overwhelming emotions that are activated and need a caring other to attune to them, to accurately assess what their needs are, to comfort and soothe them. If they receive sufficient support in this way, infants eventually learn to process their own emotions.

Rage problems are conceptualized as "the inability to process emotions or life's experiences" either because the capacity to regulate emotion has never been sufficiently developed (most common) or because it has been temporarily lost due to more recent trauma. Rage is understood as "a whole load of different feelings trying to get out at once" (Harvey, 2004)[16] or as raw, undifferentiated emotions, that spill out when one more life event that cannot be processed, no matter how trivial, puts more stress on the organism than they can bear.

Framing rage in this way has implications for working therapeutically with individuals with such difficulties. If rage is accepted as a pre-verbal, pre-cognitive phenomenon (and sufferers describe it colloquially as "losing the plot") then it follows that cognitive strategies, eliciting commitments to behave differently or educational programmes (the most common forms of interventions in the UK presently) are contra-indicated. Parker Hall proposes an empathic therapeutic relationship to support clients to develop or recover their organismic capacity to process their often multitude of traumas (unprocessed life events). This approach is a critique of the dominant anger and rage interventions in the UK including probation, prison and psychology models, which she argues does not address rage at a deep enough level.

Symptoms

One simple dichotomy of anger expression is *Passive anger* versus *Aggressive anger*. These two types of anger have some characteristic symptoms:

Passive Anger

Passive anger can be expressed in the following ways:

- *Secretive behavior,* such as stockpiling resentments that are expressed behind people's backs, giving the silent treatment or under the breath mutterings, avoiding eye contact, putting people down, gossiping, anonymous complaints, poison pen letters, stealing, and conning.
- *Psychological manipulation,* such as provoking people to aggression and then patronizing them, provoking aggression but staying on the sidelines, emotional blackmail, false tearfulness, feigning illness, sabotaging relationships, using sexual provocation, using a third party to convey negative feelings, withholding money or resources.
- *Self-blame,* such as apologizing too often, being overly critical, inviting criticism.
- *Self-sacrifice,* such as being overly helpful, making do with second best, quietly making long suffering signs but refusing help, or lapping up gratefulness.

- *Ineffectualness,* such as setting yourself and others up for failure, choosing unreliable people to depend on, being accident prone, underachieving, sexual impotence, expressing frustration at insignificant things but ignoring serious ones.
- *Dispassion,* such as giving the cold shoulder or phony smiles, looking unconcerned, sitting on the fence while others sort things out, dampening feelings with substance abuse, overeating, oversleeping, not responding to another's anger, frigidity, indulging in sexual practices that depress spontaneity and make objects of participants, giving inordinate amounts of time to machines, objects or intellectual pursuits, talking of frustrations but showing no feeling.
- *Obsessive behavior,* such as needing to be clean and tidy, making a habit of constantly checking things, over-dieting or overeating, demanding that all jobs be done perfectly.
- *Evasiveness,* such as turning your back in a crisis, avoiding conflict, not arguing back, becoming phobic.

Aggressive Anger

The symptoms of aggressive anger are:

- *Threats,* such as frightening people by saying how you could harm them, their property or their prospects, finger pointing, fist shaking, wearing clothes or symbols associated with violent behaviour, tailgating, excessively blowing a car horn, slamming doors.
- *Hurtfulness,* such as physical violence, verbal abuse, biased or vulgar jokes, breaking a confidence, using foul language, ignoring people's feelings, willfully discriminating, blaming, punishing people for unwarranted deeds, labeling others.
- *Destructiveness,* such as destroying objects, harming animals, destroying a relationship between two people, reckless driving, substance abuse.

- *Bullying,* such as threatening people directly, persecuting, pushing or shoving, using power to oppress, shouting, using a car to force someone off the road, playing on people's weaknesses.
- *Unjust blaming,* such as accusing other people for your own mistakes, blaming people for your own feelings, making general accusations.
- *Manic behavior,* such as speaking too fast, walking too fast, working too much and expecting others to fit in, driving too fast, and reckless spending.
- *Grandiosity,* such as showing off, expressing mistrust, not delegating, being a sore loser, wanting center stage all the time, not listening, talking over people's heads, expecting kiss and make-up sessions to solve problems.
- *Selfishness,* such as ignoring other's needs, not responding to requests for help, queue jumping.
- *Vengeance,* such as being over-punitive, refusing to forgive and forget, bringing up hurtful memories from the past.
- *Unpredictability,* such as explosive rages over minor frustrations, attacking indiscriminately, dispensing unjust punishment, inflicting harm on others for the sake of it, using alcohol and drugs,[18] illogical arguments.

It should be stated that anyone displaying any of these behaviours does not always have an anger management problem.

Six Dimensions of Anger Expression

Of course, anger expression can take on many more styles than passive or aggressive. Ephrem Fernandez has identified six bipolar dimensions of anger expression. They relate to the direction of anger, its locus, reaction, modality, impulsivity, and objective. Coordinates on each of these dimensions can be connected to generate a profile of a person's anger expression style. Among the many profiles that are theoretically possible in this system, are the familiar profile of the person with explosive anger, profile of the person with repressive anger, profile of the passive aggressive person, and the profile of constructive anger expression.

Causes

People feel angry when they sense that they or someone they care about has been offended, when they are certain about the nature and cause of the angering event, when they are certain someone else is responsible, and when they feel they can still influence the situation or cope with it. For instance, if a person's car is damaged, they will feel angry if someone else did it (e.g. another driver rear-ended it), but will feel sadness instead if it was caused by situational forces (e.g. a hailstorm) or guilt and shame if they were personally responsible (e.g. he crashed into a wall out of momentary carelessness).

Usually, those who experience anger explain its arousal as a result of "what has happened to them" and in most cases the described provocations occur immediately before the anger experience. Such explanations confirm the illusion that anger has a discrete external cause. The angry person usually finds the cause of their anger in an intentional, personal, and controllable aspect of another person's behavior. This explanation, however, is based on the intuitions of the angry person who experiences a loss in self-monitoring capacity and objective observability as a result of their emotion. Anger can be of multicausal origin, some of which may be remote events, but people rarely find more than *one* cause for their anger. According to Novaco, "Anger experiences are embedded or nested within an environmental-temporal context. Disturbances that may not have involved anger at the outset leave residues that are not readily recognized but that operate as a lingering backdrop for focal provocations (of anger)." According to *Encyclopædia Britannica*, an internal infection can cause pain which in turn can activate anger.

Cognitive Effects

Anger makes people think more optimistically. Dangers seem smaller, actions seem less risky, ventures seem more likely to succeed, and unfortunate events seem less likely. Angry people are more likely to make risky decisions, and make more optimistic risk assessments. In one study, test subjects primed to feel angry felt less likely to suffer heart disease, and more likely to receive a pay raise, compared to fearful people. This tendency can manifest in retrospective thinking as well: in a 2005 study, angry subjects said they thought the risks of terrorism in the year following 9/11 in retrospect were low, compared to what the fearful and neutral subjects thought.

In inter-group relationships, anger makes people think in more negative and prejudiced terms about outsiders. Anger makes people less trusting, and slower to attribute good qualities to outsiders.

When a group is in conflict with a rival group, it will feel more anger if it is the politically stronger group and less anger when it is the weaker.

Unlike other negative emotions like sadness and fear, angry people are more likely to demonstrate correspondence bias - the tendency to blame a person's behavior more on his nature than on his circumstances. They tend to rely more on stereotypes, and pay less attention to details and more attention to the superficial. In this regard, anger is unlike other "negative" emotions such as sadness and fear, which promote analytical thinking.

An angry person tends to anticipate other events that might cause him anger. He will tend to rate anger-causing events (e.g. being sold a faulty car) as more likely than sad events (e.g. a good friend moving away).

A person who is angry tends to place more blame on another person for his misery. This can create a feedback, as this extra blame can make the angry man angrier still, so he in turns places yet more blame on the other person.

When people are in a certain emotional state, they tend to pay more attention to, or remember, things that are charged with the same emotion; so it is with anger. For instance, if you are trying to persuade someone that a tax increase is necessary, if the person is currently feeling angry you would do better to use an argument that elicits anger ("more criminals will escape justice") than, say, an argument that elicits sadness ("there will be fewer welfare benefits for disabled children").[27] Also, unlike other negative emotions, which focus attention on all negative events, anger only focuses attention on anger-causing events.

As a Strategy

As with any emotion, the display of anger can be feigned or exaggerated. Studies by Hochschild and Sutton have shown that the show of anger is likely to be an effective manipulation strategy in order to change and design attitudes. Anger is a distinct strategy of social influence and its use (i.e. belligerent behaviors) as a goal achievement mechanism proves to be a successful strategy.

Larissa Tiedens, known for her studies of anger, claimed that expression of feelings would cause a powerful influence not only on the perception of the expresser but also on their power position in the society. She studied the correlation between anger expression and social influence perception. Previous researchers, such as Keating, 1985 have found that people with angry face expression were perceived as powerful and as in a high social position. Similarly, Tiedens et al. have revealed that people who compared scenarios involving an angry and a sad character, attributed a higher social status to the angry character. Tiedens examined in her study whether anger expression promotes status attribution. In other words, whether anger contributes to perceptions or legitimization of others' behaviors. Her findings clearly indicated that participants who were exposed to either an angry or a sad person were inclined to express support for the angry person rather than for a sad one. In addition, it was found that a reason for that decision originates from the fact that the person expressing anger was perceived as an ability owner, and was attributed a certain social status accordingly.

Showing anger during a negotiation may increase the ability of the anger expresser to succeed in negotiation. A study by Tiedens et al. indicated that the anger expressers were perceived as stubborn, dominant and powerful. In addition, it was found that people were inclined to easily give up to those who were perceived by them as a powerful and stubborn, rather than soft and submissive.[29] Based on these findings Sinaceur and Tiedens have found that people conceded more to the angry side rather than for the non-angry one.

Coping Strategies

Each instance of anger demands making a choice. A person can respond with hostile action, including overt violence, or they can respond with hostile inaction, such as withdrawing or stonewalling. Other options include initiating a dominance contest; harboring resentment; or working to better understand and constructively resolve the issue.

According to R. Novaco, there are a multitude of steps that were researched in attempting to deal with this emotion. In order to manage anger the problems involved in the anger should be discussed Novaco suggests. The situations leading to anger should be explored by the person. The person is then tried to be imagery-based relieved of his or her recent angry experiences.[33]

Conventional therapies for anger involve restructuring thoughts and beliefs in order to bring about a reduction in anger. These therapies often come within the schools of CBT (or Cognitive Behavioural Therapies) like modern systems such as REBT (Rational Emotive Behavior Therapy). Research shows that people who suffer from excessive anger often harbor and act on dysfunctional attributions, assumptions and evaluations in specific situations. It has been shown that with therapy by a trained professional, individuals can bring their anger to more manageable levels.[34] The therapy is followed by the so-called "stress inoculation" in which the clients are taught "relaxation skills to control their arousal and various cognitive controls to exercise on their attention, thoughts, images, and feelings. They are taught to see the provocation and the anger itself as occurring in a series of stages, each of which can be dealt with."

CBAT: An Integrative Treatment for Anger : A new integrative approach to anger treatment has been formulated called "Toward an Integrative Psychotherapy for Maladaptive Anger" published in the International Handbook of Anger. Specifically termed CBAT for Cognitive Behavioral Affective Therapy, this treatment goes beyond conventional relaxation and reappraisal by adding a variety of cognitive and behavioral techniques and further supplementing them with affective techniques to deal with the very feeling of anger. The techniques are sequenced in a contingent fashion within three phases of treatment: prevention, intervention, and postvention. In this way, people can be trained to deal with the onset of anger, its progression, and the residual features of anger.

Suppression

Modern psychologists point out that suppression of anger may have harmful effects. The suppressed anger may find another outlet, such as a physical symptom, or become more extreme. Los Angeles riots of 1992 as an example of sudden, explosive release of suppressed anger. The anger was then displaced as violence against those who had nothing to do with the matter. Another example of widespread deflection of anger from its actual cause toward scapegoating, was the blaming of Jews for the economic ills of Germany by the Nazis.

However, psychologists have also criticized the "catharsis theory" of aggression, which suggests that "unleashing" pent-up anger reduces aggression.

Dual Thresholds Model

Anger expression might have negative outcomes for individuals and organizations as well, such as decrease of productivity and increase of job stress, however it could also have positive outcomes, such as increased work motivation, improved relationships, increased mutual understanding and etc. (for ex. Tiedens, 2000). A Dual Thresholds Model of Anger in organizations by Geddes and Callister, (2007) provides an explanation on the valence of anger expression outcomes. The model suggests that organizational norms establish emotion thresholds that may be crossed when employees feel anger. The first "expression threshold" is crossed when an organizational member conveys felt anger to individuals at work who are associated with or able to address the anger-provoking situation. The second "impropriety threshold" is crossed if or when organizational members go too far while expressing anger such that observers and other company personnel find their actions socially and/or culturally inappropriate.

The higher probability of negative outcomes from workplace anger likely will occur in either of two situations. The first is when organizational members suppress rather than express their anger—that is, they fail to cross the "expression threshold". In this instance personnel who might be able to address or resolve the anger-provoking condition or event remain unaware of the problem, allowing it to continue, along with the affected individual's anger. The second is when organizational members cross both thresholds—"double cross"— displaying anger that is perceived as deviant. In such cases the angry person is seen as the problem—increasing chances of organizational sanctions against him or her while diverting attention away from the initial anger-provoking incident. In contrast, a higher probability of positive outcomes from workplace anger expression likely will occur when one's expressed anger stays in the space between the expression and impropriety thresholds. Here, one expresses anger in a way fellow organizational members find acceptable, prompting exchanges and discussions that may help resolve concerns to the satisfaction of all parties involved. This space between the thresholds varies among different organizations and also can be changed in organization itself: when the change is directed to support anger displays — the space between the thresholds will be expanded and when the change is directed to suppressing such displays – the space will be reduced.

Neurology

In neuroimaging studies of anger, the most consistently activated region of the brain was the lateral orbitofrontal cortex. This region is associated with approach motivation and positive affective processes.

Physiology

The external expression of anger can be found in facial expressions, body language, physiological responses, and at times in public acts of aggression. The facial expression and body language are as follows: The facial and skeletal musculatures are strongly affected by anger. The face becomes flushed, and the brow muscles move inward and downward, fixing a hard stare on the target. The nostrils flare, and the jaw tends toward clenching. This is an innate pattern of facial expression that can be observed in toddlers. Tension in the skeletal musculature, including rising of the arms and adopting a squared-off stance, are preparatory actions for attack and defense. The muscle tension provides a sense of strength and self-assurance. An impulse to strike out accompanies this subjective feeling of potency.

Physiological responses to anger include an increase in the heart rate, preparing the person to move, an increase of the blood flow to the hands, preparing them to strike.

Perspiration increases (particularly when the anger is intense). A common metaphor for the physiological aspect of anger is that of a hot fluid in a container. According to Novaco, "Autonomic arousal is primarily engaged through adrenomedullary and adrenocortical hormonal activity. The secretion by the adrenal medulla of the catecholamines, epinephrine, and norepinephrine, and by the adrenal cortex of glucocorticoids provides a sympathetic system effect that mobilizes the body for immediate action (e.g. the release of glucose, stored in the liver and muscles as glycogen). In anger, the catecholamine activation is more strongly norepinephrine than epinephrine (the reverse being the case for fear). The adrenocortical effects, which have longer duration than the adrenomedullary ones, are modiated by secretions of the pituitary gland, which also influences testosterone levels. The pituitary-adrenocortical and pituitary-gonadal systems are thought to affect readiness or potentiation for anger responding."

Neuroscience has shown that emotions are generated by multiple structures in the brain. The rapid, minimal, and evaluative processing of the emotional significance of the sensory data is done when the data passes through the amygdala in its travel from the sensory organs along certain neural pathways towards the limbic forebrain. Emotion caused by discrimination of stimulus features, thoughts, or memories however occurs when its information is relayed from the thalamus to the neocortex. Based on some statistical analysis, some scholars have suggested that the tendency for anger may be genetic. Distinguishing between genetic and environmental factors however requires further research and actual measurement of specific genes and environments.

PHILOSOPHICAL PERSPECTIVES

Antiquity

Ancient Greek philosophers, describing and commenting on the uncontrolled anger, particularly toward slaves, in their society generally showed a hostile attitude towards anger.

Galen and Seneca regarded anger as a kind of madness. They all rejected the spontaneous, uncontrolled fits of anger and agreed on both the possibility and value of controlling anger. There were however disagreements regarding the value of anger. For Seneca, anger was "worthless even for war." Seneca believed that the disciplined Roman army was regularly able to beat the Germans, who were known for their fury. He argued that ". . . in sporting contests, it is a mistake to become angry".

Aristotle on the other hand, ascribed some value to anger that has arisen from perceived injustice because it is useful for preventing injustice.[46] Furthermore, the opposite of anger is a kind of insensibility, Aristotle stated. The difference in people's temperaments was generally viewed as a result of the different mix of qualities or humors people contained. Seneca held that "red-haired and red-faced people are hot-tempered because of excessive hot and dry humors." Ancient philosophers rarely refer to women's anger at all, according to Simon Kemp and K. T. Strongman perhaps because their works were not intended for women. Some of them that discuss it, such as Seneca, considered women to be more prone to anger than men.

Control Methods

Seneca addresses the question of mastering anger in three parts: 1. how to avoid becoming angry in the first place 2. how to cease being angry and 3. how to deal with anger in others. Seneca suggests, in order to avoid becoming angry in the first place, that the many faults of anger should be repeatedly remembered. One should avoid being too busy or deal with anger-provoking people. Unnecessary hunger or thirst should be avoided and soothing music be listened to. To cease being angry, Seneca suggests "one to check speech and impulses and be aware of particular sources of personal irritation. In dealing with other people, one should not be too inquisitive: It is not always soothing to hear and see everything. When someone appears to slight you, you should be at first reluctant to believe this, and should wait to hear the full story. You should also put yourself in the place of the other person, trying to understand his motives and any extenuating factors, such as age or illness." Seneca further advises daily self-inquisition about one's bad habit. To deal with anger in others, Seneca suggests that the best reaction is to simply keep calm. A certain kind of deception, Seneca says, is necessary in dealing with angry people.

Galen repeats Seneca's points but adds a new one: finding a guide and teacher can help the person in controlling their passions. Galen also gives some hints for finding a good teacher. Both Seneca and Galen (and later philosophers) agree that the process of controlling anger should start in childhood on grounds of malleability. Seneca warns that this education should not blunt the spirit of the children nor should they be humiliated or treated severely. At the same time, they should not be pampered. Children, Seneca says, should learn not to beat their playmates and not to become angry with them. Seneca also advises that children's requests should not be granted when they are angry.

Medieval Era

During the period of the Roman Empire and the Middle Ages, philosophers elaborated on the existing conception of anger, many of whom did not make major contributions to the concept. For example, many medieval philosophers such as Ibn Sina (Avicenna), Roger Bacon and Thomas Aquinas agreed with ancient philosophers that animals cannot become angry. On the other hand, al-Ghazali (also known as "Algazel" in Europe), who often disagreed with Aristotle and Ibn Sina (Avicenna) on many issues, argued that animals do possess anger as one of the three "powers" in their Qalb ("heart"), the other two being appetite and impulse. He also argued that animal will is "conditioned by anger and appetite" in contrast to human will which is "conditioned by the intellect."[47] A common medieval belief was that those prone to anger had an excess of yellow bile or choler (hence the word "choleric"). This belief was related to Seneca's belief that "red-haired and red-faced people are hot-tempered because of excessive hot and dry humors."

Control Methods

Maimonides considered being given to uncontrollable passions as a kind of illness. Like Galen, Maimonides suggested seeking out a philosopher for curing this illness just as one seeks out a physician for curing bodily illnesses. Roger Bacon elaborates Seneca's advices. Many medieval writers discuss at length the evils of anger and the virtues of temperance. John Mirk asks men to "consider how angels flee before them and fiends run toward him to burn him with hellfire." In *The Canon of Medicine*, Ibn Sina (Avicenna) modified the theory of temperaments and argued that anger heralded the transition of melancholia to mania, and explained that humidity inside the head can contribute to such mood disorders.[48]

On the other hand, Ahmed ibn Sahl al-Balkhi classified anger (along with aggression) as a type of neurosis,[49] while al-Ghazali (Algazel) argued that anger takes form in rage, indignation and revenge, and that "the powers of the soul become balanced if it keeps anger under control."[50]

Modern Times

The modern understanding of anger may not be greatly advanced over that of Aristotle. Immanuel Kant rejects vengeance as vicious because it goes beyond defense of one's dignity and at the same time rejects insensitivity to social injustice as a sign of lacking "manhood." Regarding the latter, David Hume argues that because "anger and hatred are passions inherent in our very frame and constitution, the lack of them are sometimes evidence of weakness and imbecility." Two main differences between the modern understanding and ancient understanding of anger can be detected, Kemp and Strongman state: one is that early philosophers were not concerned with possible harmful effects of the suppression of anger; the other is that, recently, studies of anger take the issue of gender differences into account. The latter does not seem to have been of much concern to earlier philosophers.

The American psychologist Albert Ellis has suggested that anger, rage, and fury partly have roots in the philosophical meanings and assumptions through which human beings interpret transgression.[51] According to Ellis, these emotions are often associated and related to the leaning humans have to absolutistically depreciating and damning other peoples' humanity when their personal rules and domain are transgressed.

RELIGIOUS PERSPECTIVES

Catholicism

Anger in Catholicism is counted as one of the seven deadly sins. While Medieval Christianity vigorously denounced anger as one of the seven cardinal, or deadly sins, some Christian writers at times regarded the anger caused by injustice as having some value. Saint Basil viewed anger as a "reprehensible temporary madness." Joseph F. Delany in the Catholic Encyclopedia (1914) defines anger as "the desire of vengeance" and states that a reasonable vengeance and passion is ethical and praiseworthy. Vengeance is sinful when it exceeds its limits in which case it becomes opposed to justice and charity. For example, "vengeance upon one who has not deserved it, or to a greater extent than it has been deserved, or in conflict with the dispositions of law, or from an improper motive" are all sinful. An unduly vehement vengeance is considered a venial sin unless it seriously goes counter to the love of God or of one's neighbor.[52]

Hinduism

In Hinduism, anger is equated with sorrow as a form of unrequited desire. The objects of anger are perceived as a hindrance to the gratification of the desires of the angry person.[53] Alternatively if one thinks one is superior, the result is grief. Anger is considered to be packed with more evil power than desire.[54] In the Bhagavad Gita Krishna regards greed, anger, and lust as what leads to hell. "Similarly, anger can be controlled. We cannot stop anger altogether, but if we simply become angry with those who blaspheme the Lord or the devotees of the Lord, we control our anger in Krishna consciousness. Lord Caitanya Mahâprabhu became angry with the miscreant brothers Jagai and Mâdhâi, who blasphemed and struck Nityânanda Prabhu. Lord Caitanya wrote: "One should be humbler than the grass and more tolerant than the tree." One may then ask why the Lord exhibited His anger. The point is that one should be ready to tolerate all insults to one's own self, but when K[ishGa or His pure devotee is blasphemed, a genuine devotee becomes angry and acts like fire against the offenders. Krodha, anger, cannot be stopped, but it can be applied rightly. It was in anger that Hanumân set fire to Lañkâ, but he is worshiped as the greatest devotee of Lord Râmacandra. This means that he utilized his anger in the right way. Arjuna serves as another example. He was not willing to fight, but Krishna incited his anger: "You must fight!" To fight without anger is not possible. Anger is controlled, however, when utilized in the service of the Lord." "The conclusion is that only when we talk about devotional service to the Supreme Personality of Godhead can we refrain from useless nonsensical talk. We should always endeavor to use our speaking power solely for the purpose of realizing Krishna consciousness. As for the agitations of the bickering mind, they are divided into two divisions. The first is called Avirodha-prîti, or unrestricted attachment, and the other is called virodha-yukta-krodha, anger arising from frustration. Adherence to the philosophy of the Mâyâvâdîs, belief in the fruitive results of the karma-vâdîs, and belief in plans based on materialistic desires are called avirodha-prîti. Jñânîs, karmîs and materialistic planmakers generally attract the attention of conditioned souls, but when the materialists cannot fulfill their plans and when their devices are frustrated, they become angry. Frustration of material desires produces anger." (The Nectar of Instruction 1)

Buddhism

Anger in Buddhism is defined here as: "being unable to bear the object, or the intention to cause harm to the object." Anger is seen as aversion with a stronger exaggeration, and is listed as one of the five hindrances. Buddhist monks, such as Dalai Lama, the spiritual leader of Tibetans in exile, sometimes get angry. However, there is a difference; most often a spiritual person is aware of the emotion and the way it can be handled. Thus, in response to the question: "Is any anger acceptable in Buddhism?' the Dalai Lama answered:

"Buddhism in general teaches that anger is a destructive emotion and although anger might have some positive effects in terms of survival or moral outrage, I do not accept that anger of any kind as a virtuous emotion nor aggression as constructive behavior. The Gautama Buddha has taught that there are three basic kleshas at the root of samsara (bondage, illusion) and the vicious cycle of rebirth. These are greed, hatred, and delusion—also translatable as attachment, anger, and ignorance. They bring us confusion and misery rather than peace, happiness, and fulfillment. It is in our own self-interest to purify and transform them."[55]

Buddhist scholar and author Geshe Kelsang Gyatso has also explained Buddha's teaching on the spiritual imperative to identify anger and overcome it by transforming difficulties:

When things go wrong in our life and we encounter difficult situations, we tend to regard the situation itself as our problem, but in reality whatever problems we experience come from the side of the mind. If we responded to difficult situations with a positive or peaceful mind they would not be problems for us. Eventually, we might even regard them as challenges or opportunities for growth and development. Problems arise only if we respond to difficulties with a negative state of mind. Therefore if we want to be free from problems, we must transform our mind.

The Buddha himself on anger:

An angry person is ugly & sleeps poorly. Gaining a profit, he turns it into a loss, having done damage with word & deed. A person overwhelmed with anger destroys his wealth. Maddened with anger, he destroys his status. Relatives, friends, & colleagues avoid him. Anger brings loss. Anger inflames the mind. He doesn't realize that his danger is born from within. An angry person doesn't know his own benefit. An angry person doesn't see the Dhamma. A man conquered by anger is in a mass of darkness. He takes pleasure in bad deeds as if they were good, but later, when his anger is gone, he suffers as if burned with fire. He is spoiled, blotted out, like fire enveloped in smoke. When anger spreads, when a man becomes angry, he has no shame, no fear of evil, is not respectful in speech. For a person overcome with anger, nothing gives light.[57]

Islam

The Qur'an, the central religious text of Islam, attributes anger to prophets and believers and Muhammad's enemies. It mentions the anger of Musa (also known as Moses) against his people for worshiping a golden calf; the anger of Yunus (also known as Jonah) God in a moment and his eventual realization of his error and his repentance; God's removal of anger from the hearts of believers and making them merciful after the fighting against Muhammad's enemies is over.[58][59] In general suppression of anger is deemed a praiseworthy quality and Muhammad is attributed to have said, "power resides not in being able to strike another, but in being able to keep the self under control when anger arises."[59]

Judaism

In Judaism, anger is a negative trait. In the Book of Genesis, Jacob condemned the anger that had arisen in his sons Simon and Levi: "Cursed be their anger, for it was fierce; and their wrath, for it was cruel."

Restraining oneself from anger is seen as noble and desirable, as Ethics of the Fathers states:

“Ben Zoma said: Who is strong? He who subdues his evil inclination, as it is stated, “He who is slow to anger is better than a strong man, and he who masters his passions is better than one who conquers a city” (Proverbs 16:32). “

Maimonides rules that one who becomes angry is as though that person had worshipped idols. Rabbi Shneur Zalman of Liadi explains that the parallel between anger and idol worship is that by becoming angry, one shows a disregard of Divine Providence - whatever had caused the anger was ultimately ordained from Above - and that through coming to anger one thereby denies the hand of G-d in one’s life.

In its section dealing with ethical traits a person should adopt, the Kitzur Shulchan Aruch states:

“Anger is also a very evil trait and it should be avoided at all costs. You should train yourself not to become angry even if you have a good reason to be angry.”

Of God or Gods

In many religions, anger is frequently attributed to God or gods. Primitive people held that gods were subject to anger and revenge in anthropomorphic fashion. The Hebrew Bible says that opposition to God’s Will results in God’s anger. The Hebrew Bible explains that:

God is not an intellectual abstraction, nor is He conceived as a being indifferent to the doings of man; and His pure and lofty nature resents most energetically anything wrong and impure in the moral world: “O Lord, my God, mine Holy One... Thou art of eyes too pure to behold evil, and canst not look on iniquity.”

Christians believe in God’s anger in the sight of evil. This anger is not inconsistent with God’s love, as demonstrated in the Gospel where the righteous indignation of Christ is shown when he drives the moneychangers from the temple. Christians believe that those who reject His revealed Word, Jesus, condemn themselves, and are not condemned by the wrath of God.

In Islam, God's mercy outweighs his wrath or takes precedence of it. The characteristics of those upon whom God's wrath will fall is as follows: Those who reject God; deny his signs; doubt the resurrection and the reality of the day of judgment; call Muhammad a sorcerer, a madman or a poet; do mischief, are impudent, do not look after the poor (notably the orphans); live in luxury or heap up fortunes; persecute the believers or prevent them from praying. Islam also believes that its followers are permitted to express their personal wrath towards those who do not subscribe to their belief system.

CHAPTER 10

Anger Management

M.R. Jyothi Feddric*
Dr. R.N. Misra**

Introduction

The goal of all education is to prepare individuals for success in life and moreover success is a journey, not a destination. Since the beginning of human history we have been living under certain universal laws that have operated our daily lives whether we are aware of them or not. One of such laws is the law of correspondence, which tells that your outer world is a mirror of the inner world.

In simple words, your outer world corresponds to your inner world. What's going on around you is a reflection of what's going on inside you. One of the greatest responsibilities you have to yourself is to keep yourself thinking like a winner all day long. Certainly one will come across inevitable setbacks and disappointments of daily life and one wins upon the following situations if he/she thinks like a winner. True measure of your character is decided by your thought on what you want and what you do not want? We

* Senior Lecturer in Commerce, Government Degree College, Narasimapeta, Srikakulam District A.P.

** Prof. of Management Studies, SMIT, Berahmpur, Orissa

generally become upset, angry and lost control of ourselves when things go wrong. This is a natural tendency of most of the people, but people who have success in their life always have a winner's attitude and mentality.

They continue to think about winning and success even under the most difficult or adverse circumstances. Those who think about success and achievement all day long are basically the successful people. As per the law of the attraction, each human being is a living magnet, that we radiate thought energy and that we invariably attract into our lives the people and circumstances that harmonize with our dominate thoughts. When people think out positive and happy things, they automatically attract positive and happy people and circumstances into their lives and *vice versa.*

The choice is always up to you. One of the greatest key to positive thinking is the ability to look for good in every situation. Sooner or later, those who win are those who think they can.

Time management is an essential success skill. Managing your time effectively will help you to:

- Be more productive
- Reduce your stress level
- Improve your self-esteem
- Establish an important career skill
- Reach your goal
- Balance and successful life.

What is Success?

The meaning of success comes in many forms, and many definitions. It all depends on what you are searching for in life. Athletes may have one definition of success, and a stay at home mom may have another. A musician may see success as a number one hit, and a doctor may see success as a surgery that went well. It basically depends on the prospective of life you have. Let's differentiate between accomplishment, success and true success.

Accomplishment

It is related to the task or action that you have attempted, and the desired results obtained. It is based on what was expected, and what results were done. People accomplish things all day long, but really achieve no success in those actions.

Success

Ongoing string of accomplishments when put together, add up to a major obtainment in life is known as success. It is an ongoing realization and obtainment of worthy results, concerning actions, life wealth, or a worthy deal. It is not just accomplishment, it is beyond that. It is basically measured by the number of achievements you make. But the route which you follow to reach your goals is what actually matters.

True Success

True success is simply the realization and obtainment of a worthy ideal or result that your heart is deeply connected to it. It is what people die for it. It is a success that soaked with emotion, powered by passion, driven by destiny, and forged with the fire of the heart. That is why that, many athletes have long career. Basically their heart is attached to their success.

Success is based on what you have done with the opportunities you have been given. Success is not created in wealth or fame; it is created in the sincere attempt to reach a goal. It is destination that we must be continually striving to get to. When anyone accomplishes a goal, they have temporary success. You should set multiple smaller goals for yourself in order to reach the final desired destination. To remain successful, you must remain in motion because success never stays with you and it moves constantly. Success is a long hard road often includes many failures and trails before you reach the end.

Spend 10-15 minutes to create a one or two sentence phrase that will sum up your very own definition of success. As an example if my key success words were:

1. Freedom
2. Money
3. Peace
4. Flexibility
5. Time for time
6. Making for a difference
7. Leaving a legacy, etc.

Analyze the meaning of success from the phrase written against the words. This will indicate the next course of action to be drawn so as to reach the success point. Success can be based under the following:

I. Target
II. Focus
III. Hard work
IV. Faith/believe
V. Dedication, and
VI. Prayer.

If you want to be a teacher, that's a target and it should be with you to be successful in life. You must focus on the things/requirements that qualify you to be a teacher. So you must focus in that area to attend those qualities for you to be successful in life.

There is no short cut route to success, only it can be achieved through sheer hard work. The top of the ladder is never crowded, but only can be reached through the steps and it is the steps of hard works.

You must believe in yourself, you must say to yourself down from your heart, that you can make it, that you can pass through the turns of been a teacher. You must be dedicated in what you have determined to do in life so as to attain success in life.

Dedication is the spirit to duty. Prayer is the key to all success in life. It gives you the strength to be focused, to work hard and to be dedicated. If followed properly in our daily life and affairs, then sky is ours.

What is Time Management?

Practically speaking, time is constant; 60 seconds per minute, 60 minutes per hour, 24 hours per day and 7 days a week (24/7). It can neither be reversed nor forwarded, and moreover cannot be stored. However, the usage of time differs among each individual. Some might give time the capacity to control their lives, and others find themselves a slave of time. Some might have no time at all to relax and create a stress-free life style. But one should not make time an enemy.

Time is one of the most important resources for everyone, and sometimes most valuable. In a few case timing is everything. A sense of time can motivate, focus efforts, and get more done per hour. Time is important due the following reasons :

1. It is wisely said that if you value life, value what life is made of. Your time is your life, use it or enjoy it.
2. Time is a major function of your career. Time plays an important role in your progress and prosperity, know how to use it and you can achieve much more quickly.
3. Time is a major resource, because time itself is a raw material and knowledge of or a system of using it. If managed properly, will give rise to the optimum result as required.

There are several differences between time and other resources:

1. Time is obtained free of charge, just like the air we breath. Each morning 24 hours worth time is given to us.

2. One can never have more time than anyone else. But it is clear that some people achieve infinitely more than others in the same period.
3. Time cannot be saved and used at a later date.
4. There no substitute for time in the way that there are substitutes for other resources.
5. Every activity, no matter how small or large, requires use of commodity called time.
6. You can make better use of your own time, others can not do so, and neither can they steal it from you.

Proper use of time is a problem for many people. An excellent solution to this is to get organized through time management. Some common misconceptions about time management are:

1. Time management is common sense and does not require much effort.
2. I work better under pressure, so time management will be counter productive.
3. I do not have time for time management techniques.
4. Time management is too serious and does not leave room for fun in life. But the truth is time management is key to life and career success. Time management helps to learn more and exert greater control over your activities and life. Getting control of your time is the key to accomplishing what you want in life. Successful time management is important in all areas of life. If you can become the master of your time then you will reap the reward in both your professional and personal life. We are guilty of wasting time and putting things of till tomorrow, but the more you can effectively manage your time then the happier you will become. Instead of controlling, suppressing, or constricting your freedom, time management enables you to achieve the things you really want and frees up time to enjoy life. Every one is allotted the same amount of time in life,

that is, 24 hours in each day. You can save or steal time. You should learn how to invest it wisely. As one anonymous author said, "Time and tide wait for no one". Remember to :

- Start with yourself and analyze how you waste valuable time.
- Decide to change poor working habits by replacing them with effective tasks.
- Set yearly, monthly, weekly and daily goals and then develop strategies to reach these goals.
- Write to-do list with 80/20 rule in mind, do the most significant things first (80/20 rule is also known as Pareto rule. It is named after Vilfredo Pareto, Italian economist of 19th century. This rule states that 80 percent of all that happens at work is really the result of 20 percent effort. Most people spend 80 percent of their time trying to complete 20 percent of their tasks).

Time is your most valuable resource. Unless time is managed, nothing else can be managed. If time gets away from us, every other part of our life will get away from us, too. Time management is self management. Spend both time and money wisely so you will have plenty of each.

SOME OF THE COMMON TIME WASTERS

1. Problem : Feeling so over whelmed and anxious about your workload that you "freeze"' put things off and does not get anything done.

Solution :

1. Set priorities

2. Get started

2. Problem : *Procrastination:* Spending time on irrelevant tasks when you know you should be studying. Procrastination is the thief of time.

Solution :

1. Dividing seemingly complex tasks into smaller parts.
2. Setting up a time scale and deadline for achieving each part of a task.
3. Dealing with unpleasant task first, so that they are out of the way.
4. Action plan and prioritize your activities and tasks on a weekly basis.

3. Problem : Putting off starting a task because, it feels so overwhelming or difficult that you can not face it.

Solution : Break up the work load into small chunks.

4. Problem : Daydreaming or "drifting off".

Solution : Check your energy level and concentration. Take a short break or a little exercise every hour.

5. Problem : Feeling that you can not begin because, you won't be able to produce a perfect result.

Solution : Rather than aiming for a masterpiece each time, aim at reasonable results.

6. Problem : Poor planning.

Solution : Planning is a way of saving time for errors. Mistakes usually happen because of unexpected and unforeseen factors such as a wrong estimate of resources or new problems. With the proper plan and preparation, these unforeseen circumstances can be minimized.

7. Problem : Interruptions - telephone.

Solution : Instead of being at the whim of callers, make the phone work for you.

8. Problem : Socializing, idle conversation.

Solution : Effective conversation as per the situation demand should be adopted and followed.

9. Problem : Un-clear objectives and priorities

Solution : Set priorities as per the goal you want to achieve and the objective is to be clearly defined at the beginning of perfonning the task.

10. Problem : Stress.

Solution : Some suitable method should be followed to reduce stress of any kind. Stress is highly objectionable during performing effective tasks and hence needs special care and attention.

11. Problem : Inability to say "No".

Solution : Decide what you want to do and realistically can do and then say "no" to everything else. It is often accepted much more easily than you think.

12. Problem : E-mail and instant messenger interruptions.

Solution : Reading and answering e-mails can consume a big portion of your day. Make sure you only allow a certain amount of time for checking the mail, and then ensure that you stick to that schedule.

13. Problem : Leaving tasks unfinished, jumping from one task to another.

Solution : Complete the first task first and then move to the next task. Incase of urgency try to reschedule the time instead of jumping to the new task before the completion of first task.

14. Problem : Playing cards, games, watching television, etc. frequently.

Solution : Perform the above activities only during the time slot allotted for them.

15. Problem : Lack of self-discipline, not carrying through plan.

Solution : One should control himself as per set of rules and regulations either prepared by you or laid down by the system. Stick to the plan as far as possible unless some very urgent task comes into picture.

16. Problem : Constantly switching priorities.

Solution : Follow strictly to the priorities prepared to achieve the goal.

Effective Time Management for Achieving Success

The main benefit of effective time management is that, it can drastically improve the quality of your life. Following are the hints to effective time management :

1. Personal survey or analyze your present use of time
2. Prepare an event calendar
3. Prepare a chart of fixed commitment
4. Schedule high priority activities for peak energy times
5. Schedule most difficult activities for peak times and do them first
6. Make weekly schedule
7. Establish a regular study schedule
8. Change study subjects frequently
9. Take breaks
10. Use odd hours for study
11. Study with a partner
12. Choose study area carefully
13. List and prioritize daily goals
14. Get enough sleep
15. Make a daily check list
16. Prepare a quarterly planning grid

Conclusion

The idea of the time management has been in existence for more than 100 years. It is an art itself. It is very easy to understand but difficult to follow. To effectively manage your time, you need to follow certain values and be disciplined in all activities. It is basically a process. Keeping track of how you spend your time is not time management. Time management is about making changes to the way you spend your time. The carpenter's rule of "measure twice, cut once" equally holds good for every one of us to succeed in life. Plan your work. Take a few minutes to write out your goal and then list the steps to achieve them. Make sure to distinguish the goals that are truly important from those that may seem urgent but are really not important. If you have never managed your time before, it will take a little bit time to learn how and to do it. But just like anything else, the more you do it, the better you get. It is advised to stick with it for approximately 30 days so as to evaluate its effectiveness.

CHAPTER 11

Reasons for Anger Management

*G. Chandrayya

Anger is one of the most universal and intense emotions. Although feeling anger is normal and part of being a human being, it is a powerful emotion that can result in health problems, loss of important relationships, crimes, and destruction. Therefore, it is very important to express our anger in a way that is not destructive to others or ourselves. Anger is neither good or bad, it is a part of the normal range of human emotions. Our method of handling anger can significantly effect all aspects of our life. Some people may hold anger inside and feel tired or depressed, others may need to do something physical such as hit a wall, while others might talk it out and express it. There are many ways to express anger. When such ways become destructive to others or ourselves, it is a good time to consider making changes in the way we deal with our anger.

Reasons Why We May Get Angry

There are many different triggers that may set off anger and everyone's triggers are different. What angers one person may only mildly annoy another and vice versa. Most of Reasons likely to get angry:

* Senior Faculty Member, Government Autonomous College, Rajahmundry (A.P.).

- You or someone you love has been hurt - for example, someone criticizes you or your friend.
- You do not pass an exam or a class.
- Something has been taken away from you - perhaps a break up, the loss of a job or the death of a loved one.
- You are verbally put-down in front of others.
- Your belongings, position or property has been marred or destroyed.
- Someone cuts you off or drives erratically on the road or freeway.
- Your space has been violated. This could be someone sitting too close to you, or use of your things without permission
- You feel that a serious injustice has been done.

In each of the above cases, we may become angry because we perceive that something wrong has been done. During the seconds that our anger takes over, we do not generally stop to think about whether our anger is justified. During that time our body is probably busy going through the physiological responses to anger.

Physical Responses

Anger arises from deep in our brain, just like all of our basic emotions. It causes immediate physical changes: increased blood pressure and heart rate, dilated pupils, tense muscles, and sharper vision. These reactions occur because of the release of adrenaline, a hormone that gives us a sense of great tension and a feeling of wanting to take action. Such reactions allow us to be at our strongest and most forceful when we are in danger and need to *"act"*. Yet, because we have these same responses whether we are in danger or not, we need to be aware of them. We need to learn to identify and manage these reactions.

Dealing with Anger

A successful expression of anger allows you to release the energy of your anger at a pace in which you feel comfortable.

It also helps you to resolve the situation that created your anger, and it leaves you with a sense of calmness. There is obviously no one proper way to be angry. The way you manage your anger will be based on your individual personality. The most important priority to keep in mind in anger management is that the way you handle your anger should not be damaging to yourself or others.

Positive Outlets

Count to Ten : Pause and count to 10 or more when you are in the heat of anger and feel out of control. By forcing yourself to pause, you can break the momentum of anger and then be able to think about how you want to respond, rather than react from a strong and overwhelming physical and emotional state.

Use Delaying Tactics : When someone you know has triggered your anger, you may not be thinking clearly at the moment and can feel out of control.

Therefore, saying something such as, "I feel very upset by what you just said, and I need to think about this and discuss it with you later" allows time to think about what has happened. It also allows the person who has triggered your anger to know that you are displeased and you do intend to discuss it. Just having the self-control to delay your expression will give you more self-confidence, relief and satisfaction.

Spend the Energy : If the situation that you are in does not allow for discussion, now or later, but it leaves you bursting with anger, the fastest way to get relief is to physically release the energy. Vigorous physical activity whether hard work, or strenuous exercise, such as running, weight-lifting or aerobics can be an amazing way to release anger. Other more immediate outlets could be punching a pillow, throwing rocks at the ground or into a body of water, ripping up unimportant papers or whatever physical release you choose. Expending the energy can leave you with a general sense of relief and even calmness.

Talk It Out : If the person with whom you are angry is someone you trust, and someone you believe could vent to you in the same way, it is very healthy to talk it out after you let them know that "I am very angry" or "I am furious". Acknowledging and owning your feelings first before you talk it out helps to diffuse your anger a bit so that you can talk about what is bothering you.

Journaling : Keeping a journal in which to write down your feelings can also be very therapeutic in processing your anger.

Get Help : If you have tried time and time again to control your anger and you find that it is a continual struggle, counseling can be invaluable. A professional counsellor can help you to devise long-term strategies for dealing with chronic anger. In addition, anger management classes can be quite helpful. There is help! Remember that you are not alone! Many people struggle with learning to deal with their anger. However, the time it takes to work on dealing with your anger in a healthy and productive way is well worth the investment. As you are able to deal with your anger productively, you will find that all aspects of your life will improve, such as your relationships, your health, and your job satisfaction.

What is Anger?

Anger is a completely natural and instinctive emotion. In fact, it can be a cause for concern if a person does not experience any tinge of anger, especially when that person is subject to great duress or provocation. Angry feelings may be triggered by a person, object, incident, event or even memory. Reactions may vary from mild annoyance to aggression. However, anger has the capacity to make us say things we do not mean or do things we would not do under normal circumstances. The issue does not lie with having angry feelings but how we express it.

When does Anger become Unhealthy?

Anger becomes a concern when it becomes a lifestyle and the person develops unpredictable and destructive behaviours that affect one's quality of life. "Blowing one's top", "flying off the handle" and "blowing a fuse"; are just some familiar expressions of anger uncapped. Sulking silently in anger is as detrimental as exploding in uncontrollable rage. One's relationship, job or personal health may be at stake. Below are some tell-tale signs that one may need help with anger management:

Possible Signs of Unhealthy Anger

- Angry feelings take a long time to subside, even after the event has passed
- Feelings of anxiety or depression over inability to cope with anger
- Resorting to drugs or alcohol to curb anger
- Verbally or physically lashing out at the slightest irritation
- Family, friends or colleagues express concern over angry behaviour
- People avoid contact or interacting with the person to prevent incurring wrath
- Perpetually cynical and hostile; constantly putting others down
- Hurting another person physically or emotionally

Why Managing Anger is Important

There are health benefits in acquiring constructive ways to manage anger. As anger causes the heart beat to race and blood pressure to rise, a prolonged angry state has undesirable consequences. A person's character can be developed by possessing effective anger management skills. He or she tends to be less emotional during duress and are more focused in problem-solving. Consequently, the person enjoys better quality of social relationships.

Ways to Manage Anger

- Identify and be aware of the things or situations that could easily trigger your anger and develop coping skills to manage them. If avoiding them is not possible, refraining your thinking and attitude towards them may help. Recognise that you cannot always avoid or change the things or the people that enrage you, but you can learn to control your reactions.
- Develop the ability to express anger constructively by acquiring better communication skills through courses, training or self-improvement resources. Bottling up frustration is as destructive as letting it all out. The key is to express oneself in a way that communicates one's feelings clearly without appearing as combative or defensive.
- Deep breathing, muscle relaxation and mental relaxation are helpful in managing negative emotions.
- Engage in positive self-talk under stressful conditions. Tell yourself to stay calm, relax, and breathe easy or give yourself a pat on the back for staying cool. This is effective in preventing the anger from escalating. Using humour appropriately to defuse a tense situation is another way to gain a positive perspective of the issue.
- Walk away from potentially explosive encounters if tension is building up and staying calm and relaxed does not help. Remind yourself that lashing out in anger has great negative consequences on your physical or emotional health.
- Seeking professional counselling for uncontrolled anger is preferred over talking to family or friends.

Trained mental health professionals are better equipped to help identify areas of concern and develop anger management strategies.

- Learning to manage stress will help to reduce our frustration. Having a proper diet, getting sufficient sleep and doing physical exercises help keep stress at bay. The Health Promotion Board recommends having two servings of fruit and two servings of vegetables daily and exercising at least three times a week, at least 20 minutes each time.

One of the biggest obstacles to personal and career success is anger. When we fail to control our anger, we suffer several blows:

- Anger impedes our ability to be happy, because anger and happiness are incompatible.
- Anger sends marriages and other family relationships off-course.
- Anger reduces our social skills, compromising other relationships, too.
- Anger means lost business, because it destroys relationships.
- Anger also means losing business that you could have won in a more gracious mood.
- Anger leads to increased stress (ironic, since stress often increases anger).
- We make mistakes when we are angry, because anger makes it harder to process information.

People are beginning to wake up to the dangers of anger and the need for anger management skills and strategies. Many people find anger easy to control. Yes, they do get angry. Everybody does. But some people find anger easier to manage than others. More people need to develop anger management skills.

Develop Your Anger Management Skills

For those who have a tough time controlling their anger, an anger management plan might help. Think of this as your emotional control class, and try these self-help anger management tips:

1. Ask yourself this question: "Will the object of my anger matter ten years from now?" Chances are, you will see things from a calmer perspective.
2. Ask yourself: "What is the worst consequence of the object of my anger?" If someone cut in front of you at the book store check-out, you will probably find that three minutes is not such a big deal.
3. Imagine yourself doing the same thing. Come on, admit that you sometimes cut in front of another driver, too ... sometimes by accident. Do you get angry at yourself?
4. Ask yourself this question: "Did that person do this to me on purpose?" In many cases, you will see that they were just careless or in a rush, and really did not mean you any harm.
5. Try counting to ten before saying anything. This may not address the anger directly, but it can minimize the damage you will do while angry.
6. Try some "new and improved" variations of counting to ten. For instance, try counting to ten with a deep slow breathe in between each number. Deep breathing—from your diaphragm—helps people relax.
7. Or try pacing your numbers as you count. The old "one-steamboat-two-steamboat, etc." trick seems kind of lame to me. Steamboats are not the best devices to reduce your steam. How about "One-chocolate-ice-cream-two-chocolate-ice-cream", or use something else that you find either pleasant or humorous.
8. Visualize a relaxing experience. Close your eyes, and travel there in your mind. Make it your stress-free oasis.

One thing I do not recommend is "venting" your anger. Sure, a couple swift blows to your pillow might make you feel better (better, at least, than the same blows to the door!), but research shows that "venting" anger only increases it. In fact, speaking or acting with any emotion simply rehearses practices and builds that emotion.

If these tips do not help and you still feel you lack sufficient anger management skills, you might need some professional help, either in the form of a therapist specializing in anger management or a coach with a strong background in psychology.

How to Control Your Anger

For a person who has anger problem, learning to accept the fact is the most important. It is only after accepting the fact that we can learn to control our anger.

There are some basic forms of controlling our anger which we all can learn to acquire.

All humans experience anger so the trick is not to suppress it, instead, learn how to control anger would be the correct approach. We all become angry from time to time, and our anger can range from simple annoyance to complete rage.

Anger is often justifiable, as it prevents us from being too passive. Demonstrating our anger can also stop those irritating characters from walking over you. However, if the anger in you gets out of control, that is when you are unable to control your anger and you will blow up at the slightest irritation, it will become destructive.

It can lead to problems in your work, as well as your relationships with your close ones and friends. While there existing many anger management techniques around, there are three main techniques which you can learn and adopt it during times when you need to be in control of your anger.

The three main techniques which you can learn to adopt are to remain calm when you are angry, expressing your anger in the correct form and suppressing and converting your anger to positive energy.

When we get angry, we can express our anger in a manner which is assertive instead of aggressive. To achieve this successfully, you will first need to be aware of your needs. You will need to know how to get these needs met without harming others. When we are assertive, it does not mean that we push others around, or be overly demanding. It simply means that we respect others and ourselves at the same time. In addition to being assertive, we can also suppress our anger. Once we are able to suppress our anger, we can redirect it to something else, or we can simply convert or adopt it to our advantage.

In order to achieve the above, we need to hold our anger and think of something that is positive. Negative thinking always brings the worse out of us. It is never a bad idea to convert our anger into another form However, if we cannot convert our anger into something that is positive, we may turn this anger onto ourselves, and this can cause depression, high blood pressure and a host of other problems. There are many of us out there who is able to convert anger into positive motivation. When they are upset with themselves, they work harder to achieve their goals. This is one form of anger conversion which we can and should learn.

Anger should never go unexpressed. When we expressed our feelings, we make it known to the other party involved, and let them know exactly how we are feeling, why we are upset and how upset we are. Expressing our anger informs the other party of our current psychological status. Expressing our feeling does not necessary mean blowing our top. We can always adopt the subtle way of informing the other party of our anger. However, there will be times when the other party will counter us with anger of their own, especially if they have not learnt to control their anger correctly themselves. We must always know how to judge when to do and what to do.

There is another form of reaction for people who suppressed their anger resort to. This form of reaction instead of conversion can be very dangerous. Take for an instance, a person does not express his anger and chooses to get back to the same person who made him angry in ways which are indirect. This is a form of revenge mentally which we should learn to avoid.

How you can you handle your anger :

- Does your heart race, do your muscles tense up, or do you get a knot in your stomach? Learn how anger feels to you so you know when it's coming and can learn to control it.
- Figure out what makes you mad, and practice staying cool for the times you have to face those things.
- Calm yourself down with deep breathing, exercising, counting to 10, or other tricks that work for you.
- Double-check yourself when you get angry. If you think a friend has spread gossip about you, you may feel ready to throw the friendship away. Before you do, ask yourself if you know for sure that this is true, and tell yourself that you need to first get her side of the story.
- Stay calm and keep your voice "low and slow." You can tell people how you feel without losing your temper or fighting—and your message can get across more clearly.
- Listen to others who tell you that they are angry with you without getting upset. Ask yourself if you can see their point of view.
- Check out an anger management program at your school, community center, or religious center.
- If you feel angry all of the time, or think you are acting in ways that seem out of control or scary, talk to a trusted adult. Learning to talk about your feelings is important. Sometimes anger is really a cover for hurt feelings or other problems, and it's okay to ask for help.

Changing Your Environment

1. If you usually spend your day indoors, make a point to spend some personal time outdoors. Putter in your yard or take a walk. The fresh air will do you good, both physically and mentally.

   If you work mostly outdoors, spend some personal, private time indoors. Go home, put your feet up and andrelax.

2. If you spend the day in physical labor, give yourself a "quiet time". Sit on a park bench and watch the world go by or sit in your favorite chair and let your tired muscles relax.

   If you spend most of your day ina sit-down job, get those lethargic muscles moving! After work, take some time to walk, run, exercise to feel a surge of renewed energy in both mind and body!

3. If you spend your day in noise, make sure your "quiet time" is quiet. Give yourself a chance to calm down and clear the chaos from your thoughts.

   If you spend your day where the silence is deafening, go home and pump up the volume! Listen to the radio, play a CD, watch half an hour of television. Get your mind off your problems!

Learn to Recognize Your Anger Activators

When you're reasonably calm, take a few minutes to examine recent times when your anger flared. Jot them down. Don't relive each; just look for what triggered your anger - your anger activators. What started you simmering and when did you boil over? What effect did your temper flares have on those around you and most importantly, you? What resulted from your anger? Let this be the beginning of your anger log or anger diary.

Each day, "log" occurrences of your anger and their triggers. You'll likely find that many of the same things are making you see red everyday.

For instance, a lot of folks start each day confronted by the harsh, irritating beeping of an alarm clock. If you're one of them, consider changing its tune. Set a clock radio to music instead of alarm or purchase an alarm that starts with a quiet pulse and slowly increases in intensity.

The Serenity Prayer

You may have heard the platitude, "You're either part of the problem or part of the solution." However, to paraphrase Abe Lincoln:

"You can solve all of the problems some of the time and some of the problems all of the time, but you can't solve all of the problems all of the time."

For instance, when you experience the loss of a family member, the anger you may feel is a natural part of grieving. No matter what you do, you can't solve the problem, but you can learn to control and resolve your anger.

"God grant me the Serenity to accept the things I cannot change, The Courage to change the things we can, And the Wisdom to know the difference."

For decades, Alcoholics Anonymous and other 12-step programs have used the Serenity Prayer to help their members cope with their problems. Even if you don't believe in a higher power, you can still use this simple message as an anger management strategy to help control your anger.

If anger is affecting your relationships, your work, or your health, consider seeking help. An anger management group, class or private counseling may be your best anger management strategy. Any of these can help you develop an anger management program based on proven anger management techniques.

Anger Management Techniques

One of the greatest detriments of anger is that it makes us feel helpless and out of control. Anger management techniques aren't meant to eliminate your anger. Anger management techniques put you in charge of the situation and teach you how to make your anger work for you.

When we take the attitude that "there's no time like the present" to vent our anger and "let it rip", anger often tears huge holes in the fabric of our lives, dropping us down the rabbit hole with no way up! Anger management techniques help you learn to express your anger in constructive "ways and sew up your problems before you find yourself trying to mend fences instead.

Silly mental pictures can help diffuse anger in many situations.

Accentuate the Positive

Your partner or spouse is late again and it's making you mad as a hatter. Picture yourself at the "Mad Hatter's tea party", the White Rabbit making his entrance "I'm late - I'm always late". Surely, the Cheshire cat's smile is growing in the background as the angry dormouse shrinks back into the teapot! Why? Because your partner's tardiness just bought you some extra time!

Use the time to file your nails, read that magazine article you don't have time to read, file your nails, check your e-mail...

Put your Anger on Hold

Your partner arrives an hour late and full of excuses. You've managed to stay reasonably calm, but you can see your anger rearing its head. Say, "I know White Rabbit. Let's talk about it later and smile! You are still in control of your emotions and the situation; that's what's important. Timing is often critical to keeping anger at bay. Don't discuss issues when you're tired, or the situation has already made you irritable. Do choose a time to find solutions to problems; just make it when you can talk rationally and comfortably - when you can stay in control. Anger Management Technique #3: Let humor calm you down.

Ex: Another driver "cuts you off" in traffic. Break it down to the ridiculous. Lean back in your seat and take a deep breath. Breathe a sigh of relief that you at least still have your legs! Picture how silly you must look to other drivers, tooling down the road in your "cut off" vehicle. Parallel parking will sure be a breeze now, won't it? Anger Management Technique #4: Don't react to anger - respond. A major anger management technique is in changing the way you think and learning to respond to anger instead of reacting to it. Reacting to anger is a learned, impulsive behavior that becomes instinctive. Responding to anger allows you to examine various solutions and gives you the opportunity to choose the one that works the best for you.

Take Care of You

Make personal time each day to reflect on issues and consider solutions to problems. Work for balance in your life. Try to leave work problems at work and personal problems at home. Although we tend to often separate mind and body, they work together to make each of us into one unique being. Regular exercise, healthy eating, and adequate sleep are as essential to your emotional health *as* they are to your physical well-being.

Don't Look Back, Move Forward

Yelling, "This blasted machine never works!" doesn't make the machine work. "You're always late!" doesn't change what happened in the past and makes no plans for change in the future, except maybe for a destroyed friendship. When you put the lid on past problems, you free up time now to find solutions for current and future problems—anger management techniques to secure the lid on that grumpy dormouse!

CHAPTER 12

Interventions on Anger Management

Dr. R.N. Misra*
Dr. H. Srinivasa Rao**

Introduction

Learning to control anger is a developmental skill. The frontal cortex which is the part of the brain that controls the ability to inhibit impulses takes twenty three years to develop fully. From a developmental perspective younger children display no ability to control their anger and aggression. The typical two year old will act out all their anger. They have no ability to control their impulses—"I want it and I want it now and if I can't have it I will fight for it". Children at this stage will hit out, kick and bite.

Gradually by the time they reach school age most children can control their impulses. By the end of primary school children can delay their angry impulses and fight at times when there is no adults to prevent them, for example - pick a fight outside the gate of the school. The form of aggression is different, usually limited to punches confined to the upper body and ribs. As we move into adolescence we need to remember the pressures and the behavioural imperatives of this transitional stage. At secondary level adolescents channel

* Prof. of Management Studies SMIT Berahmpur, Orissa.
** Sr. Lecturer in Commerce Badruka College of Commerce Kachiguda, Hyderabad, Andhra Pradesh.

most of their aggressive impulses into games or competition, they either diffuse this destructive energy in sport themselves or by watching others compete.

Peer pressure, the need to conform, and the search for identity may result in risk-taking and challenging behaviours. Fighting in this age group is usually gang related. However, there are exceptions where you will see a twelve year old behaving like the two year old-acting out all their aggressive impulses and having a temper tantrum. This is a child who has never learned how to control this impulse. This student has "lost it" when you observe the tantrum. He/she is unable to hear anything you are saying and is unable to stop themselves.

What Motivates Students to Act out in an Angry or Aggressive Manner?

There are four main reasons why people act in an aggressive manner: fear that something will be taken away from them or that they will lose something they consider important; frustration at not been able to communicate in any other way; intimidation—or to bully another person into giving in; and manipulation—using temper tantrums as a way to emotionally control other people and manipulate them.

The way the student communicates and their body language is the key to identifying why they are acting in an angry or aggressive manner. They may look fearful, frustrated or threatening. The students who have never developed the skills to control their impulses and are emotionally stuck in the terrible twos usually act aggressively out of fear or frustration. With this student, teaching a programme to help them learn to control their temper, contracting for "staying in control" and redirecting them to a safe area in the build-up to the temper is the best option. Most of these children have a predictable pattern. Teachers can learn to recognise the early warning signs. Simply pointing this out to the student in a helpful way and asking what you can do so they will earn their contract can help. This all depends on the relationship you have with the student.

Some schools let the student out of class to go to the counsellor or resource teacher if they are agitated. This is all agreed and pre-arranged with clear guidelines established. Seeing problem behaviour in a developmental context gives it different meaning and implies a different type of response. Teachers typically respond with a teaching solution to a learning error, but a moralistic response to a behavioural error. In fact, behavioural mistakes are an inevitable part of learning how to behave and are developmental; what we need to do is place the emphasis on teaching student's new skills and guiding their behaviour in a positive direction. During a crisis reducing the perceived threat or helping the student to communicate can de escalate the situation.

The students who use anger to intimidate a person present as very much in control, as calm yet frightening. They make their threats or demands in a controlled manner. With these students the best thing to do is not to fight but not to give in. State the consequences of the behaviour if they follow out their threat and quote the school policy in this area. Sometimes instead of getting locked into a power battle giving a face saving way out can help diffuse the situation.

Students who try to use anger to manipulate present as calm, yet they have an inconsistent pattern of demands. The topic of conversation changes and the student may describe other incidents where they felt hard done by and begin an entirely different conversation than the one you were having. There is a clear underlying thread in this exchange: you give me what I want and I won't lose control. In this situation the broken record technique works well - simply stick to the original topic and state consequences of behaviour. It can also help to arrange a meeting at a later date to get all the concerned parties together so that all the facts are clear.

When there is good communication it is difficult to manipulate a person or situation.

INTERVENTIONS

Cognitive Behavioural Approach

The most effective approach to anger management is a cognitive behavioural approach. The cognitive behaviour theorists believe that faulty thoughts and beliefs underlie anger problems. This is a two pronged approach (1) decreasing the physiological arousal using relaxation procedure *and* (2) cognitive thought restructuring or simply changing how you think. Raymond Novaco (1975) developed a programme for helping adults to deal with anger and this has been modified for use with teenagers and children.

Relaxation training is an essential part of an anger management programme. Anger is an emotional reaction to a set of circumstances or triggers. The trigger or stressful event is known as provocation. Anger can have positive functions or negative functions. Anger can be positive as it can make us become more assertive and stand up for ourselves, it can help us express tension, and it can energise us and help us feel in control. It has negative effects when it is used too frequently, when it leads to aggression, when it is too intense, when it disrupts relationships or when it dictates the way we feel all the time.

A firework has been used as a model to explain the way anger works. The trigger is the match that lights the firework and sets off the anger response. The body of the firework is our reaction internally and externally to the event outside us, and the fuse is the mind or our thoughts about the event. There are external factors and internal factors which contribute to the explosion. The external factors we may or may not have control over e.g. stress in the classroom - too hot, too many people, someone pushing into you. The internal factors we can control. These are our thoughts, which stem from a belief we hold. The other internal factor we can control is our physical reaction to a situation. How we interpret the event can make us angry or calm us down. Our internal response stems from our beliefs and expectations in certain situations, which triggers the internal dialogue we have in our own heads.

To intervene urith a student who has difficulties with anger management first teach relaxation procedures. Next, help the student to understand that there are external events that he/she may have no control over, but that he/she can control how they think about them or how they physically react to a situation. Explain anger in terms of the fireworks analogy. The next stage is to help students track their thoughts and anger, to become aware of triggers and signs.

The mind and body are inter connected. Changing how we think can change how we feel. Changing how we interpret events by re-scripting our internal dialogue is called cognitive or thought restructuring. In anger management training this means identifying "hot thoughts" and replacing them with "cold thoughts". Hot thoughts make us more angry, and cold thoughts are thoughts which calm us down. Help the student to develop a range of cool thoughts and use comic strip style cartoons to document these. These can be written on cue cards as can a range of alternate behaviour or calming strategies. Use role play on a one to one basis, and rehearse common situations which provoke anger.

Develop a worksheet with the visual representation of the firework and have the student fill in the triggers (the match), what physically happens (body of firework) and hot thoughts which help the match ignite the fuse. With older students simply keeping a behaviour diary of situations under the headings (1) triggers—who, where, when, (2) what happened in your body and your head or what were your hot thoughts in the situation and (3) what was the outcome. This is a more age appropriate way to document anger.

Problem-Solving and Conflict Resolution

If you look at anger as a way to communicate, then the goal of intervention is to teach a more appropriate way to communicate. Problem solving and conflict resolution can be taught as alternatives to acting out behaviour. In any problem situation it is wise to begin with the use of reflective listening and non blaming *"I"* messages. Ask open-ended questions such as who, where, why, when? Closed questions close down communication.

These include stating the obvious like "do you think I can wait here all day?", "Do you think I am stupid?" Or comments like "that's too bad, well just get on with it" or "I don't want to hear it". Open questions and reflective listening skills show the student that you are listening and may help the student clarify what they want, what you want, and how it can be achieved. Closed questions are those where the student can give a yes or no answer. Knowing when to keep quiet and listen is an important skill - do not rush to give a solution but allow the students to arrive at their own solutions. Often students tell us things at times when we are preoccupied or at times when we cannot give them the hearing they need. Feel free to put the student off at the time, but arrange an appropriate time when you can listen to them later.

Simply say that what they are telling you is too important to rush and can you schedule a time to meet them and discuss it fully. Be sure to follow up on this. If they have come to you with a problem go back later and check that it has been sorted out or simply ask them how it is going. In order to problem-solve children need certain skills. First, they have to be able to recognise that a problem exists. They may need help identifying their feelings. They may have poor reasoning skills, weak logical or sequential thinking skills, or they may have poor memory. A deficit in any of these areas will make it difficult to implement problem-solving strategies. These deficits must be remedied or a way to bypass them identified before proceeding. Children who have these basic skills can solve problems but we must have faith in them and their ability to work through and find solutions. It is hard sometimes to trust that our students can make choices and decisions. This demands that we adopt the Adlerian position of driving behaviour from the back seat. In order to implement some of these ideas we have to trust and let go of some of our controlling ways in the process.

All parties must agree on the solution before it can become a plan and this is where we are able to give choices within limits. The teacher sets the limits on the behaviour. He or she structures what is acceptable in agreeing solutions. If the teacher is not open to trying the new suggestions (as long as they are reasonable) then the process will fail and the students will become discouraged.

The problem-solving technique listed here is best done one to one but can be done with a small group. It is used between teachers and pupils but students can also be taught to use the technique themselves. Problem-solving has a number of standard steps:

1. *Identify the problem :* Get everyone's view of the problem and paraphrase it. The best way to communicate a problem is to use the assertive "I" message. "I have a problem when everyone comes late to class because..." Taking ownership of the problem as opposed to saying "you are always coming late to class" in itself changes the communication. If you start by blaming then the communication goes downhill rapidly. Explain why this is a problem and request a change. If you have a solution agreeable to all, proceed to step 4. If you do not have the solution proceed to step 2. 2. Brainstorm solutions: No matter how crazy the ideas seem, take them down, write out all the possible solutions; sometimes even the craziest idea can be adapted to form part of the solution.

2. *Evaluate solutions :* Come up with a potential plan of action—everyone has to rate the listed solutions as a plus or a minus—sometimes combining two solutions can work.
3. *Agree the plan and set a time to re-evaluate it :* Agree and write out who will do what, where and when, and what will happen if they forget or do not follow through. Set a time to re-evaluate the plan. If you have a weekly or daily class meeting, state when the review will take place. A week is usually enough time to evaluate whether the plan is working or not.

It is important to keep it positive; no blaming; no criticising etc. Encourage students to participate by taking on board their comments and suggestions. Reinforce the process by praising and rewarding their efforts to resolve the issue.

Conflict Resolution

Students who are not able to negotiate often resort to conflict. To shift conflict you have to shift perceptions and this can be achieved through effective communication. Emotions play a big role in keeping the conflict going. Many people come to a situation ready to fight it out. The main emotions involved here are fear and anger. Sharing emotions can be as important as sharing perception. In order to successfully resolve a conflict, students need to feel heard, understood and empowered. Usually in conflict situations communications are poor and participants are high in suspicion. Students also need to feel worthwhile and that they are capable. The focus for them has to be letting go of mistakes and looking to the future. Students who learn conflict resolution skills develop social competencies of co-operation, empathy, creative problem solving, social cognitive skills and relationship skills. Conflict resolution encompasses negotiation, mediation, peer mediation and collaborative problem solving. There are four underlying tenets of conflict resolution:

1. Conflict is natural
2. Differences can be acknowledged and appreciated
3. Conflict when viewed in a positive way can be seen as a solution-building opportunity
4. When conflicting parties come together and build on each other's strengths to find solutions, there is a positive knock on effect where a nurturing climate is created and individual self- worth is valued.

While acknowledging how difficult it can be to resolve conflict in large groups. Wait until everyone is calm (up to 45 minutes after an incident). Use good communication skills "I" messages and no blaming. Try to get the student to see it from the other side - or the other person's point of view.

Acknowledge your part in the problem. Generate the solution or part solutions together.

Take a skills training approach outside conflict situations. Teach anger management, communication skills and use group work to develop empathy. There are very few win/win solutions so be prepared to give. Acknowledging the other person's point of view can sometimes be sufficient to shift the behaviour. It is important to stay positive and stay focused on the behaviour, not the student. In this way the student gets a clear message that this is not personal. Separating the deed from the doer can strengthen the teacher-student relationship. 5-step plan for conflict resolution similar to the problem-solving approach but with a greater emphasis on feelings:

1. *State problem :* State the problem in objective terms - the behaviour is what you can see and hear. Stay away from vague language like "Mary has an attitude" or "Johnny is aggressive."
2. *State the need :* In stating what you need from a situation and asking the student to state his or her needs, a clearer understanding can be reached which helps to shift people who are entrenched in their own point of view.

3. *Describe the feelings :* The logic behind dealing with the feelings is to get the emotions out of the way so that a rational conversation can happen.
4. *Discuss solutions :* Brainstorming is used to come up with a plan.
5. *Decide on a plan :* The steps for implementing the plan and a timeframe for reviewing the plan are decided. It is a good idea to agree the plan in writing and have all parties sign off on it.

Relaxation Training

We need to keep in mind that the mismatch, between the student's ability and the demands of the school situation can be stressful, and may produce aggression and disruptive behaviour in some. Relaxation training can also be used as a de-escalating or prevention technique. It can be adopted as part of an anger management programme or a stress management or anxiety reduction programme with older students. *Setting the Scene for Relaxation*

Often teachers have postures they ask the students to adopt as a way to calm things down. Asking the students to close their eyes and sit with their shoulders relaxed, their hands on the desk with palms facing upwards and their legs outstretched for a few minutes before beginning a lesson, can relax the mood in the class. Posture can be incorporated into drama as a key to teaching relaxation. Get a volunteer to role-play and then give the rest of the class a script which involves tension and anxiety, such as the following:

This boy is about to get the results of his test but he does not think he did well. He is sitting in his seat waiting for the paper to come back from the teacher.

The group have to tell the volunteer what posture to assume when he gets his results. This is a great learning experience. It helps to develop awareness of body language and the relationship between our thoughts and feelings and how they can manifest physically in our bodies.

Involve older students in identifying the ways they relax outside school hours. What is your own favourite way of relaxing? Why does it work? Sports, taking a bath, going for a walk are some of the common ones but it is an individual thing. Stress is part of life and having a healthy way to cope with stress is an important life skill.

We all carry tension in our bodies. A certain amount of tension in our muscles helps us to function, walk, talk, eat etc. When we are under pressure, we hold tension in certain areas of our bodies. Having the student identify where they hold tension in their body can clue them in to signs that they need to relax. With pre and early teens, use a drawing and have them mark the areas of the body where they experience stress with a pencil or marker. With older teenagers, surveying the body for signs of tension using a list is a helpful exercise.

Music can be used as a tool to build a calm atmosphere, or as background for a relaxation exercise. With adolescents, using a walkman with their choice of calming music can help them to unwind. Yoga and meditation can also be used successfully with older students. Get students to try different relaxation techniques and choose their favourites.

Students who have difficulty controlling their anger present in different ways. The key to intervention is teaching new skills, putting a strategy in place to deal with the behaviour as it occurs, not reinforcing the inappropriate or aggressive behaviour and reinforcing the student for using appropriate ways to communicate and get what they want. If a student has difficulty in a subject area we teach to it. In the same way if a student has a problem controlling his/her anger we should teach to this also. The interventions discussed—cognitive behaviour therapy, problem solving, conflict resolution and relaxation have wider applications. These are life skills which are relevant for all students and not just those with problems controlling anger. Finding the time to teach these skills can be a challenge but thirty minutes of prevention is better then two hours of fire fighting. A proactive approach is better then a reactive one..

CHAPTER 13

Anger Management and Its Methods

Dr. R.N. Misra*
*R.K. Misra**

Introduction

Anger management is a process of learning to recognize signs that you're becoming angry, and taking action to calm down and deal with the situation in a positive way. Anger management doesn't try to keep you from feeling anger or holding it in. Anger is a healthy, normal emotion when you know how to express it appropriately. Anger management is about learning how to do this. Although you can learn how to control your frustrations by practicing anger management techniques on your own, the most effective approach is to take an anger management class or to see a mental health counselor.

Why it's Done

Anger management helps you recognize frustrations early and resolve them in a way that helps you express your needs—and keeps you calm and in control. Coping well with anger is a learned behavior, just as behaving badly when you get frustrated is a behavior you have to unlearn. Anger management is a way of systematically recognizing what

* Prof. of Management Studies, SMIT, Berahmpur, Orissa.
** HR Manager, Banglore, Research Scholar.

pushes your buttons and how to respond in ways that work for you instead of against you.

Everyone feels angry and says and does things he or she regrets from time to time. This is normal, and not necessarily a sign you need to seek out anger management help. However, when your anger is damaging your relationships, is making you miserable or is resulting in dangerous or violent behavior, you probably need help.

Some good indicators you need help controlling your anger include:

- Often feeling like you have to hold in your anger
- Frequent arguments with your partner, children or co-workers that escalate frustrations
- Trouble with the law
- Physical violence, such as hitting your partner or children or starting fights
- Threats of violence against people or property
- Out-of-control behavior, such as breaking things or driving recklessly

What You can Expect

Anger management classes or therapy for anger management (also called psychotherapy) can be done one-on-one, with your partner, child or other family members, or in a group setting. You may need to attend a number of classes or counseling sessions over a period of weeks up to a few months.

- Generally, counseling for anger management focuses on learning specific skills and ways of thinking to cope with anger.
- If you have any other mental health conditions, such as depression or addiction, you may need to work on these other issues for anger management techniques to be effective. The aim of counseling and anger management classes is to teach you to:

- *Identify situations that are likely to set you off* and respond in nonaggressive ways before you get mad.
- *Use specific skills* to use in situations likely to trigger your anger.
- *Recognize when you aren't thinking logically* about a situation, and correct your thinking.
- *Calm yourself down* when you begin to feel upset.
- *Express your feelings and needs assertively* (but not aggressively) in situations that make you feel angry.
- *Focus on problem solving* in frustrating situations—instead of using energy to be angry, focus on resolving the situation.

Results

Improving your ability to manage anger has a number of benefits. You'll feel like you have more control when life's challenges turn up the heat, and more relaxed in challenging situations. Knowing how to express your feelings assertively means you won't feel frustrated because you feel like you need to "hold in" your anger to avoid offending someone. Anger management can help you:

- *Argue less :* Enjoy better overall communication that results when you talk about your anger rather than letting it build. This will help you avoid saying impulsive and hurtful things that damage relationships with family members, friends and your partner.
- *Maintain better health :* The stress caused by ongoing angry feelings can increase your risk for health problems, including headaches, sleep problems, digestive problems, heart problems and high blood pressure.
- *Prevent psychological problems* linked to anger, which can include depression, problems at work and troubled relationships.

- *Use your frustration to get things done :* Anger expressed inappropriately can make it difficult for you to think clearly, and may result in poor judgment. Learn to use feelings of frustration and anger as motivators to work harder and take positive action.
- *Help avoid addictive escapes :* It's common for people who feel chronically angry to turn to alcohol, drugs or food. Rather than using alcohol, drugs or food to dull anger, you can use anger management techniques to keep your cool and your control.

Methods of Anger Management

Psychologists recommend a balanced approach to anger, which both controls the emotion and allows the emotion to express itself in a healthy way. Some descriptions of actions of anger management are:

- *Direct,* such as not beating around the bush, making behaviour visible and conspicuous, using body language to indicate feelings clearly and honestly, anger directed at persons concerned.

  Honourable, such as making it apparent that there is some clear moral basis for the anger, being prepared to argue your case, never using manipulation or emotional blackmail, never abusing another person's basic human rights, never unfairly hurting the weak or defenseless, taking responsibility for actions.
- *Focused,* such as sticking to the issue of concern, not bringing up irrelevant material.
- *Persistent,* such as repeating the expression of feeling in the argument over and over again, standing your ground, self defense.
- *Courageous,* such as taking calculated risks, enduring short term discomfort for long term gain, risking displeasure of some people some of the time, taking the lead, not showing fear of other's anger, standing

outside the crowd and owning up to differences, using self-protective skills.

- *Passionate,* such as using full power of the body to show intensity of feeling, being excited and motivated, acting dynamically and energetically, initiating change, showing fervent caring, being fiercely protective, enthusing others.
- *Creative,* such as thinking quickly, using more wit, spontaneously coming up with new ideas and new views on subject.
- *Forgiveness,* such as demonstrating a willingness to hear other people's anger and grievances, showing an ability to wipe the slate clean once anger has been expressed.
- *Listen* to what is being said to you. Anger creates a hostility filter, and often all you can hear is negatively toned.

A common skill used in most anger management programs is learning assertive communication techniques. Assertive communication is the appropriate use of expressing feelings and needs without offending or taking away the rights of others. It is typically started with the use of "I" statements followed by a need statement. For example, "I feel upset when you don't take my feelings into consideration when you talk about your past relationships. I hope you can be more thoughtful and know what you should and should not say the next time."

With regard to interpersonal anger, Dr. Eva L. Feindler recommends that people try, in the heat of an angry moment, to see if they can understand where the alleged perpetrator is coming from. Empathy is very difficult when one is angry but it can make all the difference in the world. Taking the other person's point of view can be excruciating when in the throes of anger, but with practice it can become second nature. Of course, once the angry person is in conditions of considering the opposite position, then the anger based on righteous indignation tends to disappear.

Signs of Anger and How to Manage Them in Sobriety

Angry feelings are one of the greatest challenges for recovering alcoholics and addicts. Relapse is often related to the inability to constructively handle anger. Mismanaged anger poses a threat to recovery for the newcomer and the old-timer. Sometimes the greatest threat is to relationships. In this article, we're going to identify anger signs, identify the causes, decide how to react, and also learn how to prevent and prepare for situations rather than get angry about them. *Identifying and Dealing with Anger.*

Identify Your 13 Anger Signs:

- Headache, stomachache and backache
- Rapid speech
- Yelling and screaming
- Sarcasm or cynicism
- Denial or rationalization about your behavior
- Revenge fantasies
- Thoughts about drinking or using drugs
- Arguing with others
- Becoming silent or withholding
- Avoiding Others
- Isolating
- Becoming Violent
- Compulsive eating, spending, cleaning, or sex.

Recognize Angry Feelings:

- How does your anger show?
- Do you deny your anger and hide it?
- Do you acknowledge your anger and deal with it constructively?

Identify the Cause:

- What is the situation?
- Who is involved?
- Is this the first time, or is this a pattern?
- What other feelings are you experiencing?
- Are you too stressed? Tired? Hungry? Lonely? Scared?

Decide How to React:

- Reason with your angry self-talk.
- Change thoughts. From: *"Pm angry at you because you..."* To: *"It's unfortunate this happened, but it's not worth the price I pay."*
- Do physical activity. Engage in exercise that involves large muscle groups, like arms and legs to release pent-up energy that can fuel anger. Walk, jog swim, dance.
- Engage in physically demanding work. Chop wood. Clean the yard, garage, attic. Build something.
- Talk directly the person involved.
  - o Use a calm and assertive voice tone.
  - o Practice listening.
  - o Don't interrupt. Be as polite as you would be to someone you didn't.
  - o If you're too angry, practice first with a third party. Talk to a friend, a relative, a therapist, or a religious leader. Use the internet to find discussion communities. Several communities online have members who will help you think through a situation and what you can say. Find communities that are well moderated by reading posts from other people before you join. Pick a community that is supportive and respectful, and which protects your identity by asking you to participate with another name, such as the one in this *Self-help Magazine.*

Avoid behaviour that will make the situation worse:

- Artificial stimulants such as nicotine and caffeine. Remember that decongestants and stimulant drinks such as Red Bull can also give you a surge of energy that can be easily misplaced when angry.
- *Ranting and raving.* Unlike conventional wisdom dictates, it is often best NOT to say whatever is on your mind. While it is important to express yourself, taking the time to find respectful yet honest statements to represent your feelings.
- *Name-calling.* This is simply childish and the result is likely to only be destructive.
- Compulsive behaviour with food, money or sex.
- *Stomping out the door.* If you need to leave, excuse yourself without blaming the other person, with statements such as "Please excuse me. I am afraid I will say something that I can regret later." Tell the other person when you will return, such as, "I'll go take a walk to calm myself down and we can talk when I come back in an hour, ok?" Be sure to get a response, and speak in a civil tone, or you may well return to someone is closed to you advances.

Prevention and Preparation

- Meditation can help balance the nervous system, and contribute to less stressful anger management.
- Daily attention to diet and exercise will improve focus and concentration.
- Keep a log of your anger work, including triggers, behavior and future planning.
- Chart your progress and be generous with self-praise when you change your behavior.

Only you can decide on the best method to use at this time to handle your anger. Of the alternatives your have, which seem the best? What are the possible outcomes if you try a particular alternative? What will you do if this alternative doesn't work? Write in a journal. Discuss it with a friend or sponsor. Bring it to your recovery or therapy group. Seek professional help when needed. And remember, anger is NOT bad. It is a normal and healthy human response!

How to Control Anger Problem

Anger is normal emotion that each individual has. Everyone is subjected to get angry with something or someone. The only difference is how an individual control anger problems. Anger only becomes a problem if it's already out of control and becomes harmful or dangerous to anyone. Anger can be controlled easily if we've learned these few tips.

First thing that an individual with anger problems needs to consider is the harm that is caused by anger. Uncontrolled anger can be very dangerous if it's out of control. An individual's way of thinking is dysfunctional. Many people were harmed because of uncontrolled anger and even caused someone's life. As the statement say, "Think before you act." If you feel angry and if you want to control it, you need to pause for a moment and take a deep breath to help you relax so you can think and react positively.

Second, try to divert your thoughts. You can find something to read; humorous books or magazines, watch television, or listen to relaxing music that you like. I know these three ways are really good in diverting someone's thought quickly. This is a very helpful ways to control anger problems.

Third, will be prayer. I know this may sound awkward or silly but it works for me. If you feel angry, try to offer a silent prayer. Prayer gives us comfort, calms our mood, and peace in our mind. You don't need to speak if you're praying. You can just pray through your thoughts and heart. Try this and you'll be surprised that it works. This is the method that really works for me when I'm trying to control my anger problems. It also makes us closer to God and chance to increase our faith in Him. In our prayer we can ask for help and strength to overcome our angry feelings. Indeed, you will feel better after. Most people are ignoring this method to control anger problems because they feel awkward and shy, that's normal if you're not used to it, but if through practice you'll get used to it and will find it more effective than any anger method that you know of.

These are just few of those simple methods to control anger problems with ease. Guaranteed, that if you try to do these simple methods, I know that it will have a positive result after, and you will see that you were able to control your anger without any harm done.

How to Move Beyond with Anger

People make mistakes and do things that hurt and disappoint us all the time. And we make mistakes and hurt and disappoint others as well. If we are to maintain our relationships, we need to learn to move beyond our anger over the mistakes and unpleasantness of others. We can't do anything to change what has happened in the past, but we can change how we think about it, including choosing not to think about it at all. We have to learn to move beyond anger and sadness not only for the good of our relationships but also, just as importantly, for our own health and happiness. Harboring negative feelings is bad for our health and only hurts us. It doesn't serve the situation in any way. So we learn to forgive and forget for ourselves, because it is the only sensible thing to do-not to hold on to negative thoughts and feelings, which are also bound to create more pain and hurt in the future for others, possibly even people who had nothing to do with our pain. When we allow ourselves to be involved in and feed our negative thoughts and feelings, chemical reactions take place in the body that are detrimental to our health, we make ourselves unhappy doing this, and we make those around us unhappy as well. This suffering is so unnecessary once you realize the effects of doing this, how fruitless doing this is, and that there is another way to handle such thoughts and feelings.

We are used to thinking of our thoughts and feelings as ours. They seem to belong to us. But the truth is that our negative thoughts and the feelings that arise from them are part of the human condition; they are part of how the human creature we are responds to life. The beauty is that, even though we are in a human body, we are not human, but spirit, or consciousness, that has taken human form. Mastery of the human condition is seeing this great truth, that although we are human and are programmed to have negative thoughts and feelings, they are part of our humanity, not our essential self, or Essence. Our essential self is, in fact, what is reading these words and capable of choosing to believe the thoughts that go through the mind or not. We can choose to express the more primitive programmed responses of negativity and anger or not. We are all evolving to becoming free of this human programming, which causes so much suffering within ourselves and on this planet. The way to move beyond anger and other harmful emotions is to see that they are generated from within us by what we tell ourselves about a situation: "He shouldn't have done that," "That's unfair," "How could that have happened!" "She must not love me," and so on. We tell stories about what other people do that cause us to feel hurt, offended, wronged, and consequently angry. These stories are the source of our anger. Without them, there would be no anger, no matter what life brought us. This is the great truth that can set us free from the suffering caused by our human programming. Whether you suffer or not is in your hands! This is immensely freeing, and seeing this stops the violence and negativity from extending to others and being sent around the world. When you stop creating anger and hurt within you, you also stop creating it outside of yourself, and the planet needs this now. The earth needs peace, and it starts within each of us.

Moving beyond anger is a matter of ignoring negative thoughts and not acting on negative feelings. If you are experiencing anger or other negative feelings, then allow them to be there, without either trying to get rid of them or expressing them. Be with those feelings with the compassion of your true self. Be curious and discover what you just told yourself that created those feelings. And then see that no matter how true that thought might seem, it is not true that someone or something should be different than he or she or it is-because it's already too late for that! It is the way it is. And then see that hanging on to those thoughts and feelings is only harming yourself and can't do anything to change what is. From this place of compassionate acceptance, you can become free from the negativity and return to peace, which is what you and everyone else really wants. You can have your self-righteousness, revenge, and anger if you want, but ultimately these only harm yourself. You have the power to make another choice, and the more you exercise your power to choose love and acceptance over anger and other negative emotions, the easier it becomes to remain untouched by adversity and human-generated storms.

Anger Management You can Control

These are the ways you will learn how to deal with anger management in this article:

- Learn how to use the energy "rush" of anger in a positive way.
- If something makes you angry, it's because you care-that's good!
- Habitual displays of anger shut down communication from others.
- Anger management is a set of readily available skills, building on simple strategies like "time-out".
- Learn tactful, understanding responses that prevent confrontation from escalating.

For starters, everyone gets angry, but as a society we pretend that only wicked people get angry, and in their out-of-control emotionality, they do terrible things. There isn't even a polite way to express anger. Anger is a little guilty secret that troubles nearly everyone, a universal emotion that no one seems to know how to handle properly.

Let's start by admitting that anger has its good, and useful, side. First, it tells you that you really care about whatever the subject is that has your blood boiling. If you don't care about something, are truly indifferent to it, it just can't make you angry! Secondly, anger presents you with an impressive burst of energy-lots of power to fix the problem, make a change, or solve a difficulty. But all we usually do with that energy burst is throw something and yell. So, again, here's a secret—a powerful resource at our disposal, if only we knew how to use it.

Third, anger is a very complicated thing. Sometimes it's connected with jealousy, with guilt, with frustrated wants, with fear, and with hurt. Sometimes it comes on quickly and sharply, other times it's more like a slow simmering. People have different levels of "normal" anger, the attitude they carry around all of the time. Those who are often impatient, frustrated, on their guard against being cheated, expecting bad things to happen, feeling watched all the time, those people carry a high level of anger, and it doesn't take much of an event to cause an explosion. Still others who are usually sad, jealous, resentful, disrespectful of others, insecure, and have feelings of worthlessness, also carry high levels of anger.

We know from medical research that making a habit of angry feelings is very unhealthy, leading to many potentially deadly diseases. Not only is habitual anger horrible for your own health, it's tough on all those around you, too. They will tiptoe around you, or avoid you altogether, fearing that any attempt at honest communication will trigger a war. They feel cheated out of a good relationship with you people who cause this reaction in others have a harder time getting hired, are rarely included in invitations, and aren't sought out for leadership positions. And since they are ready to blame others for everything, they just take their isolation as proof that everyone's against them. What a sorry existence!

One sure sign of out of control anger is a temper tantrum. Have you ever had one of those? Did it help make the problem better? Probably not, if my experience is any guide. When I was little I had quite a temper, and my cousin Jack, a little younger than me, was often the victim of it. One time I even put him in a wheelbarrow and threw it off the garden wall!

Well, in spite of my temper, Jack survived and grew up - way up - he became over six feet tall. One summer not long after we were grown, I visited him at the family's cabin in the Adirondack Mountains, and he was so nice. He took me out in a canoe. Of course, half way across the lake, he stood up. That's an impressive sight, a six-footer standing in a canoe. He started to rock, and said very sweetly: "Linda, remember that wheelbarrow?" Was that lake ever cold! It seems it's true that what goes 'round comes 'round, and your behavior comes back to bite you!

If you ever, in anger, feel as if you're going to do something as foolish as throwing a person off the garden wall, maybe it would help you to know that there are some pretty fool-proof ways to manage anger. The most widely known, is of course, the time out. Count to ten, take a break, develop a sudden coughing fit and have to go get a drink of water. Give yourself some time to get your emotions back under control.

There are some other tips just as useful. Ask yourself how important, in the long run, that thing that's making you angry is. Will it matter terribly five years, weeks, or minutes from now? Getting some perspective helps you calm down. You can remind yourself that the person who is behaving in a way that you respond to with anger is probably doing and saying what seems best to them at that time. People can only behave in ways that are consistent with their knowledge and their desires, so maybe trying to understand that person's information and wants will help you be more compassionate and less angry.

Another very powerful strategy for managing anger is to strengthen yourself so that you're not so vulnerable to it. Take good care of your body, use mini-relaxations to help you think more clearly and less rigidly, practice meditation or prayer frequently, and set your mind on positive things to crowd out the negative. Each and every time you find yourself becoming angry, stop and calmly decide whether you're going to allow that emotion to take control of your life, even for a few minutes. If the decision is no, then have some well-practiced, considerate responses ready to deflect the anger, both yours and the other person's. You might say, "My experience is different", or "You may be right, at that", or "I can see how you might feel that way".

None of these responses commits you to their viewpoint, nor do they insult the other person. If you decide that you want to experience and use the energy that anger gives you to make a bad situation better, then use all your skill for that purpose, rather than for destructive ends. In the long run, you'll be proud of yourself, others will be impressed, and you'll be developing rapidly in wisdom and understanding.

Guidelines of Anger Management

Difficulty handling anger is one of the most common problems for survivors of brain injury. Several reasons for this are: (1) increased frustration and irritability; (2) increased pain; (3) distractibility; (4) depression; (5) lack of work, leisure activity, sex, sleep.

Also, depending on the area and nature of the brain injury, sudden, explosive outbursts for no apparent reason or with no prior warnings can also occur. These can sometimes be managed with medications such as Tegretol, Inderal, Lithium, tranquilizers, or anti-depressants.

The following guidelines can also help in overall management of anger:

- Identify sources of stress and provocation.
  * What are your current ways of dealing with problems, how can you develop more effective ways of dealing with them?
  * Develop a realistic understanding of your limitations and modify expectations of what you can do.
  * Work on prioritizing important matters from trivial ones.
  * Enlist an objective third party, or "sounding board" to help evaluate your problem-solving strategies.
- Practice stress reduction/relaxation techniques.
  * Learn to identify or "tune into" early warning signs of anger (e.g. muscles tensing, increased heart rate, face flushed, etc.) This also includes angry thoughts ("That's it, I've had it", "I'm going to tell that s.o.b. where he can go", etc.)
- Take care of yourself.
  * Get adequate rest
  * Find a physical outlet (swimming, walking, etc.)
  * Eat nutritionally
  * Cut down on caffeine
  * Eliminate alcohol or other mind—altering non-prescription drugs
- Develop social outlets.
  * family/friends
  * support groups
  * Examine assumptions about others and their motivations—consider alternative explanations for others' behavior. Without enough facts, we tend to fantasize.
- Try to find the humour in situations—don' take things personally!

- Individual counseling can help you deal with depression, losses, sexual frustrations, adjustment issues, and manage stress.
- Develop more realistic and useful standards for evaluating quality of life—these will most likely be different from what society dictates. Areas to look at are:
  * work and productivity
  * love
  * play
  * beauty
  * male/female roles
- Give yourself permission to daydream/ fantasize!

Remember, anger in itself is a valid felling, and frequently is a signal for change—either within oneself or in a relationship. There will be times when expressing anger is necessary in order to make change happen. Keeping anger bottled up inside is not healthy for both emotional and physical well-being. Some points to remember for expressing anger in a constructive manner are:

- Identify source of anger—be sure it is directed at the appropriate person.
- Did you perceive the problem accurately?
- If possible, rehearse your strategy beforehand.
- Choose the right time and place. Give yourself time to cool off before speaking.
- Avoid exaggeration (use of words such as "always" or "never").
- Stick to the issue-avoid "kitchen sinking".
- Focus on the incident itself, rather than a personal attack ("You are so stupid").
- Be ready to make concessions-you can't always win. Be prepared to say, "I'm sorry", or "I was wrong", and work at "forgiving and forgetting".

Index